Tracing Invisible Lines

Electracy and Transmedia Studies

Series Editors: Jan Rune Holmevik and Cynthia Haynes

The Electracy and Transmedia Studies Series publishes research that examines the mixed realities that emerge through electracy, play, rhetorical knowledge, game design, community, code, and transmedia artifacts. This book series aims to augment traditional artistic and literate forms with examinations of electrate and literate play in the age of transmedia. Writing about play should, in other words, be grounded in playing with writing. The distinction between play and reflection, as Stuart Moulthrop argues, is a false dichotomy. Cultural transmedia artifacts that are interactive, that move, that are situated in real time, call for inventive/electrate means of creating new scholarly traction in transdisciplinary fields. The series publishes research that produces such traction through innovative processes that move research forward across its own limiting surfaces (surfaces that create static friction). The series exemplifies extreme points of contact where increased electrate traction might occur. The series also aims to broaden how scholarly treatments of electracy and transmedia can include both academic and general audiences in an effort to create points of contact between a wide range of readers. The Electracy and Transmedia Series follows what Gregory Ulmer calls an image logic based upon a wide scope—"an aesthetic embodiment of one's attunement with the world."

Books in the Series

KONSULT: Theopraxesis by Gregory L. Ulmer (2019)
Exquisite Corpse: Art-Based Writing Practices in the Academy, edited by Kate Hanzalik and Nathalie Virgintino (2019)
Tracing Invisible Lines: An Experiment in Mystoriography by David Prescott-Steed (2019)
The Internet as a Game by Jill Anne Morris (2018)
Identity and Collaboration in World of Warcraft by Phillip Michael Alexander (2018)
Future Texts: Subversive Performance and Feminist Bodies, edited by Vicki Callahan and Virginia Kuhn (2016)
Play/Write: Digital Rhetoric, Writing, Games, edited by Douglas Eyman and Andréa D. Davis (2016)

Sites

Gregory Ulmer's *Konsult Experiment*: http://konsultexperiment.com/

TRACING INVISIBLE LINES

AN EXPERIMENT IN MYSTORIOGRAPHY

David Prescott-Steed

Parlor Press
Anderson, South Carolina
www.parlorpress.com

Parlor Press LLC, Anderson, South Carolina, USA

Printed in the United States of America on acid-free paper.

S A N: 2 5 4 - 8 8 7 9

Library of Congress Cataloging-in-Publication Data on File

978-1-64317-075-6 (paperback)
978-1-64317-076-3 (hardcover)
978-1-64317-077-0 (PDF)
978-1-64317-078-7 (ePub)

1 2 3 4 5

Electracy and Transmedia Studies
Series Editors: Jan Rune Holmevik and Cynthia Haynes

Copyeditor: Jared Jameson.
Book design: David Blakesley

Parlor Press, LLC is an independent publisher of scholarly and trade titles in print and multimedia formats. This book is available in paper, cloth and eBook formats from Parlor Press on the World Wide Web at http://www.parlorpress.com or through online and brick-and-mortar bookstores. For submission information or to find out about Parlor Press publications, write to Parlor Press, 3015 Brackenberry Drive, Anderson, South Carolina, 29621, or email editor@parlorpress.com.

Contents

Acknowledgments

First and foremost, I would like to thank Julie and Olive, the two most important people in my life. I am very grateful for your love, understanding, and endless support of my artistic preoccupations. Whatever disposition this project describes, and whatever creative outcomes might serve best to express it, nothing is as important to me as the life we are making together. I love you more than the moon and the stars in the pristine Heathcote sky.

In the creative fields, I would like to acknowledge the wonderfully multifarious organism that is the experimental music community here in Melbourne. It is an honor to be a collaborator with, and not infrequently a student of, the many artists whom I call my friends and peers.

I would also like to express my sincere gratitude to Kevin Wisniewski and Felix Burgos, editors of the imaginative and eclectic journal *Textshop Experiments*. Their support for my forays into creative and critical thinking has helped fuel the momentum needed for me to undertake this much larger project.

Tracing Invisible Lines

"We speak of the abyss when, having been separated from a basis of support and having lost a point of support, we go looking for one on which to rest our feet."

—Martin Heidegger

1 Mystoriography: Theories and Considerations

As a writer, sound artist, and design-arts theory teacher living in Melbourne, Australia, I appreciate how important it is to seek out new material and theoretical tools for developing a creative practice, whether with the aim of enhancing its perceived social function or simply as a means of advancing its esthetic qualities. The image of the artist as a person chipping away at a project by themselves, an isolationist's approach to conceptualizing what it might mean to make art in a studio space of some form, is a fairly limited depiction of what it means to make art. It may be deemed rather romantic in its implicit appeal to individuality and, thus, in its claim to authenticity. To the extent that it is imagined, it is an artificial image, and one anchored in a specific socio-historical context. As David Inglis explains:

> The "magical" power of certain people, such as art critics, gallery owners and patrons of the arts to define what counts as "art" and what does not, is a phenomenon peculiar to modern societies in the last 200 years or so. Before that, no-one had seriously entertained the view that "art" and "everyday life" were totally separate from each other. The terms "art," "artwork" and "artist" are *historical inventions* primarily of the nineteenth century. Before then, these terms did not exist. . . . Indeed, the ideas of "art," "artworks" and "artists" are not just *modern* inventions but are specifically *Western* inventions too. Societies outside the West have not historically possessed these categories and the ways of seeing cultural products that they encourage. (91)

If we accept the socio-political and economic argument that we exist in a multi-cultural and globalizing industrial society, it seems strange to remain dedicated, in our thoughts and actions, to Western attitudes around art, specifically, the notion that art and life are discrete modes of existence that come together only in the lives of small groups of special people, people who have somehow been born with an artistic gift that makes them far more suited to a life of "making" than the rest of the general population and which, in turn, might find them less suited to the quotidian tasks of day to day living. How can this distinction be made when life is itself a creative process of trial and error, when it is filled with our efforts to build relationships and to establish meaningful roles in the communities that we value, in which we may perform our identities and learn from other people?

Despite this question, I cannot claim to have the most articulate and insightful answer to it. I can remember when I was a child, however, my parents telling me: "Life is hard. You need to make something of yourself. You need to make something of your life." They wouldn't say it simultaneously, as a synchronized voice, like two oscillators of a synthesizer (whereby a master oscillator resets the cycle of the slave), but their individual statements have conjoined in my memory to form a single adult voice declaring possession of universally applicable insight. It is an adult concept that probably seemed harsh to my immature, child-like ears, though I infer it carried with it a work ethic and an emphasis on self-reliance, on personal responsibility, and that this was part of an education deemed necessary by parents who wanted to raise an adult and not a voting child. It took me several years, but eventually I found a way to make sense of these kinds of authoritative self-assertions, something more workable than just stern warnings about the grueling nature of a long and inflexible life that, thus, I imagined stubbornly awaited me, as if the world itself was an authority from which I should learn to protect myself, to become ever more articulate at self-defense. When I finally moved past this species of anxious, paranoid thinking and reached a place of emerging cultural agency, when I started focusing on my creative strengths, less on what pre-existed to challenge me, but rather what I could create as a challenge to myself that was sharable with others, I gradually realized something that has remained with me ever since. I realized that, from quite an early age, I had been trained in line with the world-view that the most important thing in life was *making*, that life was a *making-process*, and that, in order for it to hold value, this process demanded my sustained and conscientious engagement.

My formative environment was not only my home-world, but the social and mass-media contexts to which I was exposed. Focusing on the home, however, here I made a sideways glance at a lesson about the importance of living an artistic life; of recognizing life as a creative opportunity; and of the importance of making my effort visible to others, the importance of sharing a creative outcome with a community, of making it available for public response and debate, and that this somehow added value to the work process, to the verified usefulness of the labor effort itself.

The idea that the domestic life prepares a person for social life is nothing new. It is an understanding that we can trace all the way back to the enlightenment feminist Mary Wollstonecraft. Wollstonecraft was the original Feminist; her classic book of feminist philosophy *A Vindication of the Rights of Women* was published in 1792 at the time of the French revolution when the rights of man were under negotiation, for want of a better phraseology. She believed that women deserved an education that would enable them to carry out, to their fullest potential, their responsibilities that included the education of their children and being proper companions to their husbands: "civilised women of the present century, with a few exceptions, are only anxious to inspire love, when they ought to cherish a nobler ambition, and by their abilities and virtues exact respect" (6).

It stands to reasons that, in the socio-political context of the same-sex marriage debate, which at the time of writing is on my mind because a bill for the legalization of same-sex marriage was only yesterday passed by the Australian Senate, the matter of who chooses to perform what role in the home, if roles are even defined, is a complex issue that attracts vigorous and passionate debate. For me, however it might be that consulting adults choose to relate to each other, this does not change Wollstonecraft's underlying recognition about the dynamism present in home-life that sets the stage for everything beyond it.

Wollstonecraft's advocacy for the recognition of the fundamental role of the home in formulating the adult-to-be has not gone out of date. We are still talking about how important a stable home is for the long-term well-being of an individual, not least of all their mental well-being (Perkins). In this sense, the domestic space can be taken as a metonym of a greater state of play, a broader image of everyday life encapsulated in the social constructionist understanding that humans are products of a complex social fabric. Our "events, realities, meanings, experiences and so on are the effects of a range of discourses operating within society" (Braun and Clarke 9). In view of this idea, it is important to take stock of our conditions to inform and enrich the social value of whatever acts of communication our projects entail that, in my case, might bare some vague resemblance to that modern, Western category called *art*, however burdened this word is with historically anomalous bourgeois values. Whatever the right word might be for that part of life in which things are made for the purpose of reflecting critically upon it, when I stop to consider what might need to be done to evolve my artistic development, not wanting to speak for the needs of other creative people, I am looking for activities that facilitate investigation into, and learning about, the multifarious "tensions between individual spontaneity and the work-process relationships on which society is based" (Macey 75). In this multi-cultural and globalizing society, in which the institutionally prejudicial classifications and evaluations of art are always open to revision, I recognize, as I suspect many artists do today, the importance of finding critical distances from which to reflect upon, and further motivate, the practice I am pursuing.

In using the term *critical distance* I am referring to intellectual and material spaces that exist somehow outside of one's familiar art-making context that can be accessed and used to facilitate new insight into that activity. For example, the tried-and-true art-historical narratives of the modernist avant-gardes focus, at least as far as it has been articulated in the context of tertiary visual-arts-related education, have been ocularcentric; there is a tendency to focus on the sculptures and paintings and other visual artefacts that have been produced by figures belonging to the German Expressionists, or the Futurists, for example. In such cases, occupying points of critical distance could mean taking a moment or two to listen to, and discuss with a community atmosphere, the sound-based works that such movements have produced [I am thinking of Luigi Russolo's *Intonarumori* (1910–30) or what has, by Nordic Black Metal musicians, been cited as a key source of their esthetic inspiration—Edvard Munch's *The Scream* (1893–1910), which is proto-typically Expressionistic]. Occupying a point of critical distance means having found, information beyond what one already has at hand so that they can enrich their understanding—further energize artistic production.

Critical distance can be achieved in a variety of ways, depending on one's own skills, time, and resources. Today, what many of us have at our disposal, which we use when we want to go looking for information, is the Internet. It makes sense, then, that I should draw attention to the information superhighway now, in explaining how, while surfing the Web one day, browsing online cultural studies and arts-related videos in search of presentations or discussions relating to experimental, creative research methods, I spent some time on YouTube listening to a lecture at Massachusetts Institute of Technology (MIT), delivered remotely by American media theorist Gregory Ulmer [Vardouli, "Gregory L. Ulmer on Mystoriography (*Teletheory*, 1989)"]. It seemed to me that the lecture was being transmitted by webcam from his workspace to a screen in an architecture classroom at MIT, evidence (the video itself) dictating that during this time the lecture was being recorded onto a digital device, the file of which would subsequently needed to have been transferred onto a computer, perhaps compressed into a lossy file format, before being uploaded to a YouTube channel in 2014, which I then watched on my own computer in Melbourne, Australia, almost two-and-a-half years later. Therein, Ulmer is another instance of the very media data he has spent his academic career investigating: "We are in an image, now, and should feel our way around this scene" (Ulmer "The Chora Collaborations"). Although not quite a sentient computer, Ulmer piques our interest with his evaluation, set against late modern society's historically anomalous and disorientating capacity to self-transmit across virtual space in real time.

Ulmer's MIT presentation on creative responses to media culture drew attention to the power of imagination and invention, to the relevance of the intellectual, emotional, and cultural comprehension of personal experience, as well as a wariness of the limits of sequential logic. I listened to Ulmer talk about the theory and practice of the *mystory*. On several occasions I found myself dragging the time-slider back to review frames and past seconds of speech, to hear again Ulmer's explanation of how mystoriography provided a platform by way of which people may uncover a form of personal metaphysics and an insight into their *creative disposition*. In the French language, the words are the same (*disposition créative*) though, in lieu of *disposition*, Ulmer employs the word *dispositif*, which can be traced to Michel Foucault's interview *The Confession of the Flesh* (194):

> What I'm trying to pick out with this term is, firstly, a thoroughly heterogeneous ensemble consisting of discourses; institutions; architectural forms; regulatory decisions; laws; administrative measures; scientific statements; philosophical, moral and philanthropic propositions—in short, the said as much as the unsaid. Such are the elements of the apparatus. The apparatus itself is the system of relations that can be established between these elements.

What ensemble of tendencies and idiosyncrasies would lead a person to think carefully about mystoriography? Perhaps an ensemble that would take to heart the ancient Greek philosopher Socrates's dictum that the unexamined life is not worth living, uttered at his trial for corrupting the youth of Athens, a crime for which he was sentenced to death by the forced consumption of hemlock.

> If on the other hand I tell you let no day pass without discussing goodness and all the other subjects about which you hear me talking and examining both myself and others is really the very best thing that a man can do, and that life without this sort of examination is not worth living, you will be less inclined to believe me. Nevertheless that is how it is, gentlemen, as I maintain; though it is not easy to convince you of it. (Plato 71–72)

Ulmer is well aware of Socrates's predilection for critical thinking—a shared cognizance as to the importance of prolonged, self-critical evaluation—quoting Socrates directly in the opening minutes of his MIT lecture's Q&A section (Vardouli "Gregory L. Ulmer [Q&A] on Mystoriography"). The practical model with which Ulmer associates this ancient idea is the mystory. The anticipation and ideal is that, once a person completes a mystory and gains insight into their disposition—into the ensemble of socio-cultural contexts in which they are embedded and entangled—they may use this insight to inform and empower their creative praxis, approaching creative projects with a renewed sense of self-authenticity and existential purpose.

By the time I happened upon Ulmer's presentation, Socrates's attitude towards the unexamined life was already familiar to me, reiterated in the *philosophy on the streets* projects of Alain de Botton (*The*

Consolations of Philosophy, *The Architecture of Happiness*, *Essays in Love*, *Status Anxiety*), and ever present in the conversational dialogues that comprise Astra Taylor's documentary film *Examined Life*.

Having happened upon Ulmer once again, against this ancient philosophical backdrop, the mystory appealed to me; it captivated my imagination. I accept that this appeal had as much to do with my creative, my humanitarian, and, in this sense, my non-competitive side as it had to do with my ambitious, aspiring side—to my willingness to participate in competitive behavior. The thought of mastering my own creativity in some way, of gaining personal empowerment through a clarification procedure, is motivating. If Ulmer's concept of the mystory could provide me with a theoretical structure and suggested practical approach that could not only be used as a means to develop a kind of writing, but also as fuel for future artistic activities not limited to writing, this was something I wanted to be a part of.

My interest in Ulmer's subject matter was piqued when he mentioned having gained extensive experience with using mystoriography in the classroom. As a professional artist teaching at a tertiary level in the design-arts, with some post-graduate design-arts supervision experience behind me, I am always on the look-out for creative, investigative activities that might be of benefit to the students I talk with. Institutionally, we are still a long way off from incorporating the mystory exercise into our existing curriculum. Nevertheless, at least as a starting point, I was willing to offer myself up as a kind of guinea-pig—as a way of testing the proverbial waters of a non-conventional scholarly assemblage. By the time Ulmer's uploaded lecture was over, I had decided to develop my own mystory, embarking upon it in the spirit of adventure (excitement mixed with trepidation), and make it available should anyone wish to read it.

On this note, there are limits to the assumptions I can make about the use-value this book might have for other people; active readers will be able to ascertain this value for themselves. Nevertheless, given the pervasive focus on arts-related practice, it makes sense that this book will appeal to artists and scholars with an interest in critical approaches to creativity. In the general sense, this book contributes to a discussion about the learning journey that a person might navigate along the way to articulating their own creative purpose in a contemporary context. It exposes the importance of engaging intellectually, emotionally, and practically in the socio-cultural and historical factors that continue to inform one's practice (i.e., that art never occurs in isolation and that undertaking socio-cultural and historical inquiry is a vital aspect of art-making when our ambitions lie beyond the merely decorative and in unknown spaces, where the consciousness of making getting lost is an entirely acceptable outcome). As Rebecca Solnit says, at the front end of her book *A Field Guide to Getting Lost* (4), "Leave the door open for the unknown. That's where the most important things come from, where you yourself came from, and where you will go." Solnit recalls a workshop that she led, at which a student arrived carrying a quote from the pre-Socratic philosopher Meno: "How will you go about finding that thing, the nature of which is entirely unknown to you?" This question made a lasting impression on Solnit, who recognized that the task of answering questions of the self requires artists to extend beyond their own boundaries, branching into unfamiliar terrain. "The job of artists," she writes, "is to open doors and invite prophesies, the unknown, the unfamiliar" (5). One might say that the task of all art is to defamiliarize, to show aspects of the world in a new light, to transform them in a way that furthers understanding, that provokes a learning experience in the viewer. This book shares Solnit's philosophical mood with its a hunger for transformation and so has something to offer other such hungry artists.

Specifically, the book's emphasis on sound-based practice sees it opening a door between the sonic arts and the field of electracy; through its addition of sound and music to the genre, this book extends the scope of studies into Gregory Ulmer's work beyond English literature and the ocularcentric arts. This critical difference means that the book will be of interest to many students and scholars working in the design-arts, offering them a new handbook for sonic conceptual art practice.

But please be aware; whatever variety of creative dispositions a mystory might exhume, I can say now with utter certainty, knowing what I do myself, that I'm not one to jump, without a second, third, or even a fourth thought. However much enthusiasm I have for long walks in dark spaces, before anything more, it seems fitting to reflect on some of the theoretical nuances of Ulmer's concept, and include these here in a gesture of preparation for whatever twists and turns might be ahead.

It would be inaccurate to say that developing a mystory is all about garnering creative control, though a sense of mastery is a reasonable outcome to anticipate. To focus too greatly on control would be to feed a limited appraisal, one that gives attention to only half of the whole; I shall address an unavoidable, if welcome, element of uncertainty and indeterminacy in a moment—when making comment on the observational parallax that arises from the fallibility of the human memory. For now, however, Gregory Ulmer's concept of mystoriography provides us with a model of approach to the praxis of creativity, that is, to how we actively and conscientiously navigate our creative interests and impulses, and how we make sense of these personal aspects in light of the socio-cultural contexts in which they are experienced. Then, with this clarity of direction in mind, make physical efforts to innovate energized acts of invention in a material reality. In Ulmer's words, "[a]n experiment in mystoriography derives its guidelines from the sciences and arts of our time, just as 'history' was invented in keeping with the naturalistic tenets of nineteenth-century science and art" (*Teletheory* 44). Mystoriography seeks to "recognize the peculiar configuration of possibility in one's own moment [by] designating the nexus of history, politics, language, thought, and technology" (Ulmer *Teletheory* 82). "Such an approach to history," explains Byron Hawk, "is grounded in our particular, local experiences of time and place and looks to map them to larger, global histories through a new form of writing" (238).

The historical context in which we find mystoriography positioned, a space of radical negotiation that is dedicated to elucidating, reimagining, and reconfiguring in an improvisational, almost aleatoric manner the cultural/cultivated self, is given further form and color by a neuroscientific circumstance. In his MIT lecture, Ulmer recounts a neuroesthetic theory that the human imagination is grounded in just four or five key images that have become embedded in the brain from childhood [Vardouli, "Gregory L. Ulmer on Mystoriography (Teletheory, 1989)"]. I later found that this idea comes from the studies of creativity conducted by scientist Gerald Holton and American psychologist Howard Gruber. It is worth reproducing, in full, an elucidation Ulmer offers in the course of his email interview with Sergio Figueiredo:

> Heuretics (electrate pedagogy, post(e)-pedagogy) opens up this position of taste or personal judgment, style, manner, to make it as rich and complex as the position of expert schemata. The historian of individual creativity in science, scholars such as Gerald Holton and Howard Gruber who study individual creativity, identified this neglected dimension as that

> of predisposition or propensity of an individual. Logic and empirical testing are obvious dimensions of scientific practice. Creative approaches add predisposition: recurring themes transversing epochs and apparati. These patterns are found in individuals and collectives alike. Persons in the process of creative performance apply predispositions formed in childhood development that have nothing to do with disciplines but that guide the imaginations of the learner. Mystory (which is to electracy what historiography is to literacy) is the pedagogical genre that includes predisposition in learning, formalized in the Wide Image, the phrase introduced by Gerald Holton referring to the three or four fundamental images organizing the imaginations of learners. (72)

Thanks to the availability of Darwinian manuscripts since the 1950s, Gruber had the opportunity to "explore Darwin's development through the lens of cognitive psychology" (in Gruber and Bödeker 110). Gruber observed the centrality of the tree/coral motif in the work of Charles Darwin, noticing how enduring the image of living nature as a tree had been throughout the work that Darwin produced up to and including his *On the Origin of the Species*, starting with his *First Notebook on Transmutation of Species*. According to Gruber, the tree of life sketches, drawn by Darwin in his notebooks only fifteenth months prior to him "solving the major problems of his theory," enabled Darwin to represent "the fortuitousness of life, the irregularity of the panorama of nature, the explosiveness of growth and the necessity to bridle it 'so as to keep number of species constant'" (in Gruber and Bödeker 248). Darwin's tree of life—his image of wide scope—looked to be the driving force of his imaginative output.

Likewise, Gruber observed how central the image of the compass was in Albert Einstein's work (Einstein had taken great delight in the magnetic field of the compass that his father had given to him as a boy), observing also the image of crashing waves outside Virginia Woolf's nursery. Adding to this, Gruber noticed the tower motif that reoccurs in the work of Irish Poet W. B. Yeats (Yeats bought a Norman Tower in 1917, which he called "Thoor Ballylee" and that became his home in 1919, though the tower motif was already present in Yeats's work (e.g., *A Prayer for My Daughter, Ego Dominus Tuus, The Phases of the Moon*), as well as Mozart's image of pacing. In each case, what Gruber found interesting was that an image from childhood had apparently evolved over the course of the creator's life to inform their life-long work; the image of wide scope constituted the imaginative themata by which the stimuli of the world seemed to have been translated and from which a notional truth of the universe had been esthetically construed—what Ulmer calls a "personal metaphysics" [in Vardouli "Gregory L. Ulmer on Mystoriography (Teletheory, 1989)"]. As Gruber says:

> An image is wide when it functions as a schema capable of assimilating to itself a wide range of perceptions, actions, ideas. This width depends in part on the metaphoric structure peculiar to the given image, in part on the intensity of the emotion which has been invested in it, that is, its value to the person. (135)

Intellectual and emotional comprehensions of the world take place on a spectrum of imaginative abstractions that germinate like a hybrid plant in a garden shed that the gardener may forget about only to return weeks or months later to see what it has grown into; perhaps it has died and decayed, transforming in the dark organic matter that provides the soil with nutrients for future cultivations.

Gerald Holton was also interested in the idea of the wide-scope image. As William Endres explains, following Holton's "studies of people who showed exceptional creativity in their work and lives, like Albert Einstein . . . [Concurring with Gruber] Holton observed that these people tend to have a central image that directs their thoughts and notions of life, that determines the playground of their imaginations" and which "Holton proposes people develop by the time they reach the age of eighteen" (78–79).

Images of wide scope are an important discovery in the study of creativity. They seem often to mark the first surfacing into a concrete form of the inchoate, emotional, and sensory qualities of a creator's vision; the first materializations of vision into the consensual world where creative products must ultimately be made. Once deposited into reality, images of wide scope serve as levers and scaffolds for building the actual creative products (Briggs 194).

Images of wide scope form the nuclei in the complexities of the imagination that emerges in the course of a person's lifetime to drive inventive activity and lend thematic color to other images, other memories. They comprise the bedrock, the centrifuge and, thus, the fixed hypothetical axis around which all other images orbit and to which they ultimately refer, like the magnetic force of a compass that drives the needle northward.

Building upon the work of scientists like Gruber and Holton, Ulmer reiterates Einstein's compass metaphor in his MIT lecture, describing the component parts of the human imaginary as needles that can be analysed in terms of what they signify about a person's creative disposition. I will consider this in more detail later, as I start to build my own mystoriography. Presently, I would like to extend Ulmer's metaphor, taking a moment to acknowledge another type of signifying needle, one that accounts not for place but, rather, for motion through space. What I have in mind is the speedometer needle that provides visual feedback to the driver of a vehicle as to how fast he or she is traveling. This is an important alternative to acknowledge because it offers another layer of comprehension to our current idea of axial images around which all subsequent images rotate. In Ulmer's rendition, we can move about in our situation, whether this be physical, social, cultural, or otherwise, all the time doing so with compass in hand, and all the while noticing the needle shifting in its relative position on the dial as it relentlessly seeks a northern cardinal point, its disposition, magnetism. This is the relentless drive that Ulmer calls an *invariant principle*.

It is a compelling metaphor, but one that says very little about how the rate at which we encircle, how fast we move in our socio-cultural, material circumstances, that is, the velocity of our creative rotations and recollections or, rather, our impetus and *momentum*: "the strength or force that allows something to continue or to grow stronger or faster as time passes" (Merriam-Webster). To unpack this detail further, we can liken the experience of moving intuitively and non-linearly through memories to the practice of the dérive, as described by the *Situationist International* of Post-WW2 Paris and theorized by leading figure Guy Debord: "One of the basic situationist practices is the *dérive*, a technique of rapid passage through varied ambiences. Dérives involve playful-constructive behavior and awareness of psychogeographical effects, and are thus quite different from the classic notions of journey or stroll" ("Theory of the Dérive" 62).

> Entre les divers procédés situationnistes, la dérive se définit comme une technique du passage hâtif à travers des ambiances variées. Le concept de dérive est indissolublement lié à

> la reconnaissance d'effets de nature psychogéographique, et à l'affirmation d'un comportement ludique-constructif, CE qui l'oppose en tous points aux notions classiques de voyage et de promenade. (Debord "Théorie De La Dérive" 62)

A key word found in the English translation is *rapid*, an adjective, thus a modifier of the noun *passage*, a fast-moving object such as a train, bus, car, or even a person moving, guided by association, through their own imagination and memory. In Debord's French text the word *hâtif* is used, denoting a hurried state of play, as in hurried work, but that can also mean *hasty*, as in the context of a decision or judgement. Interestingly, there is a familiar quality here, in the lightness of touch with which Ulmer would like us approach a mystoriographical exercise—to not think too much about it: "Let the mystory tell you" [Vardouli, "Gregory L. Ulmer on Mystoriography (Teletheory, 1989)"]. This lightness of touch calls for a friendly, relaxed, and non-exact disposition.

It is in an attempt to affect a lightness of touch that I might come unstuck—in large part due to my love of minutiae, an anxiousness around my own language use, and my tendency to spend extensive periods of time alone while working on self-directed, relatively demanding activities—activities structured in such a way that I may perambulate in a free and improvisational manner, drifting productively. Thus, it seems worthwhile to mention the Situationist detail because of the element of speed that is central to the practice of orientation and disorientation, and this is what leads me to think about the kind of needle that might signify, not direction, but rather velocity (i.e., a speedometer of one's own creative drive).

As anyone who has sat in the front passenger seat of a car, truck, or other passenger vehicle, when we glance over to see how fast our driver is going, perhaps alerted by an apparent and sudden increase in the roar of the engine, glancing over and seeing the needle from a non-exacting angle, observing it at parallax, we may be forgiven for thinking that they are driving faster than they really are. This assumption could lead the passenger to voice a complaint, to ask the driver to slow down a bit, and the driver might protest in response, doubtless that he or she is driving within the legal limit. The passenger might look at the needle again and feel convinced, in their displacement, that the vehicle is running ten miles over, maybe even more. Just as the needle of the speedometer is seen at parallax by the passenger, can we not apply this thinking to the perception the driver will experience of the environments, the ambiences, through which they are traveling? The Situationists spoke of moving quickly through the streets of Paris, and from this we can say that they were activating psychogeographical insight conditioned, at least in part, by their velocity. We all work at our own pace, as befits our disposition; it is not always possible or advisable to skim across the surface.

I have approached the notion of velocity, but in doing so, by way of the manner of imaginative association that I hope Ulmer would appreciate, I have arrived at the notion of parallax—derived from the Greek word *parallaxis* (παράλλαξις), meaning *alteration*. With this in mind, let's return to neuro-science to summarize how the human memory works; after all, whatever the founding images of our imaginations are, they are only ever remembered across the distance between the present moment, itself never static, and whenever they originally occurred. A mystoriography, to the extent that it is built upon personal memories and their relationship to political, linguistic, imaginative and technological histories, and however we might embellish or enrich data with contemporaneous information, is grounded in the act of remembering. The problem, as Mount Sinai School of Medicine neuroscientist Daniela Schiller explains, is that "[e]ach time you retrieve a memory it undergoes this storage process. . . . We don't really remember the original; we remember the revised version" (Young Rojahn). Schiller is sharing an established neuro-scientific understanding that can be traced back to the psychologist Frederick Bartlett. In 1932, Bartlett showed "that in the process of remembering humans rely on summaries or 'schemes' of the past—when a person 'recollects' what happened, he or she will reconstruct a memory from these schemes, often adding or changing details" (Research Institute for History). The act of remembering does not bring into the present an image of the past but, rather, a non-exact reflection of its previous recollection, an alteration, a distortion. Each time we remember, we reinforce that memory's trace, making it stronger in comparison to other memories, thus changing or perverting it in some way. For example, thinking momentarily about my early schoolroom experiences, I can say that I am currently remembering not the bullish primary schoolteacher, but my previous recollection of her, a recollection that took place perhaps only seven days ago, albeit itself occurring more than thirty years after the interactions that info established the uncomfortable impressions of her that have remained with me all this time. We are talking about a vast stretch of time during which that teacher's personal brand of pedagogical terrorism may have been remembered hundreds of times, with each instance taking the imagination further and further away from the truth of what occurred and deeper and deeper into the mood and fiction that arose from it. As reflective of a general human condition, we can say that, across time and space, the perception(s) we generate of our creative disposition, of our invariant principle must, in principle, remain variable, open to negotiation, vulnerable to corruption, subject to radical doubt in the sense that, as British Sociologist Anthony Giddens says: "Modernity institutionalises the principle of radical doubt and insists that all knowledge takes the form of hypotheses: claims which may very well be true, but which are in principle always open to revision and may at some point have to be abandoned" (*Modernity and Self-Identity* 3).

Giddens goes on to discuss "systems of accumulated expertise," and we cannot exclude self-comprehension from the complete range or scope of things we can claim to have knowledge of (*Modernity and Self-Identity* 3). It would seem that the mystoriographical method is an exercise in parallax, and that this is the nature of the associative path to which Ulmer has frequently referred. There is enough inexactitude, for me, in this circumstance so that, by taking a heavy-handed approach, I can at least aim to thoroughly articulate a revisable narrative (i.e., show as best as I can what remains open to change).

Ulmer acknowledges that the creative disposition unearthed through mystoriographical activity is not fate, not destiny. Rather, identifying the practice of engaging with one's *themata* (a set of ideas that drive creativity) — integrated composition, disposition, compass — is "a way to imagine one's creative disposition in the world," providing a context of behavior in light of which one thinks and acts independently in the world [Vardouli, "Gregory L. Ulmer on Mystoriography (Teletheory, 1989)"]. With this denial of fate and destiny, Ulmer recognizes the individual's scope for producing future, alternative mystoriographies that might bare similarities with, or differ from, their previous incarnations, mimicking the fallibility of memory in this way, producing and reproducing its cognitive projection, its veritable ghost. No; the mystoriography does not exclude revisionary praxis. But this is a matter for the future, and I am not currently concerned with this domain; I am thinking explicitly about the present, its unstable relationship to the past, and that this instability is a precondition for any mystoriographical attempt whatsoever. While we can be sure of the intention of a mystoriography, in its partial reliance upon memory, it inherits this instability, this parallax and paradox, and so is destined in this way, we might say, to remain caught in an ellipsis, a precarious orbit around a fundament of creative thought that is continuously being erased by the act of thinking itself. The ideal object is never seen directly, only by reflection, by refraction, and by re-inscription, by an over-writing. I don't think there's any denying this, or any unmanageable problem associated with it. It is perhaps what makes creative thinking so appropriate here, given that it offers hope to an exhumation, permitting the freedom to imagine the identity of memories found even in advanced stages of decay that, in turn, is a freedom to demonstrate personal choice when it comes to self-identification (i.e., when it comes to the task of articulating who one is right now). There is a basic human requirement that we approach the tell-tale signs forensically and with success. A mystoriography draws no small amount of strength, and vital life, from this uncertain and unpredictable condition. It aligns closely with Ulmer's interest in creative logic, which is associational, free browsing, low focus (as analogous to hyper media network), sensitive to pattern and, thus, a modality of creative thinking that differs from narrowly focused, sequential reasoning [Vardouli, "Gregory L. Ulmer on Mystoriography (Teletheory, 1989)"]. This is not a green light to proceed without care; rather, it is an invitation to proceed without fear or inhibition.

There is a literary analogy to what I have just said that is found in the form of Alain Robbe-Grillet's *nouveaux romans* (e.g., *Jealousy*, *In the Labyrinth*, *Repetition*) that, in their phenomenology of pure surface, negotiate worldly scenes forensically. Though lacking confirmation, because of his recognizable esthetic sensibility, I suspect (in the absence of any verification beyond esthetic clues) that Ulmer already shares my admiration for Robbe-Grillet's forensic and parallaxical approach to memory, or else certainly could. Robbe-Grillet's books seem at odds with psychology; there is a frustration affected by Robbe-Grillet's apparent "absence of any attempt at psychological analysis or any use of the vocabulary of psychology, total rejection of introspection, interior monologues, 'thoughts,' or descriptions of states of mind; and a systematic use, almost like that of music, of 'objective themes,' including a network of stains" (Morrissette 9). Ulmer's mystoriographical method, although akin to Robbe-Grillet in its sensitivity to patterns, and the nuanced changes to these that evolve through their repetition, through revisionary practice, embraces the psychological realm (in its embrace of affective states and displays), with the apparent result being an amalgamation of neuro-science and cultural reflexivity. Here, I understand reflexivity in the terms laid out by Anthony Giddens, who defines the reflexive project of the self as a bidirectional relationship between self and society that "generates programmes of actualisation and mastery" and that helps initiate "'Life-politics'—concerned with human actualisation, both on the level of the individual and collectively" (*Modernity and Self-Identity* 9). Likewise, mystoriography fosters an opportunity to energize a dynamism between self and society, marking an effort to access the emotional or affective parts of personal and collective human experience, while accounting for the central role media (including but not limited to digital media) plays in mediating (in transporting and translating) this bidirectional relationship. It is useful to think of the mystory, therefore, as a culturally reflexive method that foregrounds creative novelty and play and thus directs us, like a compass, in the direction of authentic, creative innovation. The notion of *authenticity* is incredibly loaded in its meaning and implications, attracting great scepticism under a post-modern epistemology, for it assumes a hierarchy relating to truth claims about the self. We are folding back into previous acknowledgements about the welcome limitations of the mystory. I should say, however, that there is honesty in this, honesty about its limits, clarification that it does not presume the existence of a unified and centered identity, and that making the context of honesty communicable means that it is no less useful.

We speak directly to Ulmer's theory when noting that each person is in the best position to conduct their own mystoriography because he or she occupies the best position from which to critically identify and evaluate their own creative disposition, their invariant principle, however obliquely one may stare back at it through the lens of their own creative work and as a recipient of institutional feedbacks. He or she is ultimately responsible for investigating, communicating, and putting this disposition into practice. No one can do it for them without betraying the legitimacy of the process (pushing the case for a critical auto-ethnography). Ulmer is informed by neuro-esthetics; we have seen neuro-science challenge the accuracy of our perception. Perhaps, then, it is appropriate to think of the two metaphors again: neuro-science puts us as odds with the invariability of the compass needle, at least in terms of the metaphorical function that Ulmer has ascribed to it, with the result being that we are hailed always into the mood of indirectness, into the realm of indirect objects. We may accept the model of the compass as denoting an ideal, but it is worth elucidating parallax as the lived-experience (i.e., first-hand experience). In this way, we can remain mindful of the sites of displacement from which we attempt to comprehend ourselves, and on the grounds of which we creatively contribute to a material reality—like human language thrown from a labyrinth. I think that this is why the image is so important in the process of creating a mystory, that is, of encountering and of dealing with this troubling thing called memory. As W. G. Sebald put it:

> The photograph is meant to get lost, somewhere in a box in an attic. It's a nomadic thing, that, you know has a small chance only to survive. And I think we all know that feeling when we come accidentally across a photographic document being of one of our lost relatives, being of a totally unknown person, and we get this sense of appeal. They're stepping out, having been found by somebody after decades or half centuries. Having been found by somebody, all of a sudden, they come stepping back over the threshold, and they say "We were here too once." (in Taller de Escritura Fuentetaja)

There is something to be learned from Sebald in terms of the poetics of the image and the mood by which we memorialize our own pasts through reiterated, albeit flawed, recollections. The image plays a central role in the creative negotiation of a reflexive praxis, and maybe there is something of our own selves that is meant to get lost in a box in an attic, that is nomadic to the extent that it cannot be pinned down in the seemingly boundless psychological space where all lost things seem to go until they are found again, hypothetically perambulating as in the Situationist dérive. It might be accidentally uncovered and, thus, resemble Freud's uncanny in its disconcerting dissolution of the boundary between fact and fiction, troubling us with a long forgotten image of ourselves. The self of the past, therefore, might well be what steps out and asks for our attention, not in a narcissistic or vain way, but rather simply to say, this is where you come from—a statement that invites you and challenges you, therefore, to make some meaning from it. There will likely be times when the mystory also strikes the creative researcher as belonging to "that class of the frightening which leads back to what is known of old and long familiar" (Freud 220). Although the unreliability of memory may be troubling, perhaps because it does not promise the security that we expect (and that we might seek in other areas of our lives: family, relationship, career, housing, etc), the brain is always learning, and to learn we need change; the brain needs to change in order to evolve. Relating this back to our key focus, perhaps it can be said that mystoriographical method leads an individual to produce a creative and composite trace of, or perambulation through, such change—a representational (partial, incomplete, metonymic) account of their own socio-cultural, and technologically driven, life-narrative, still ongoing.

Parallax; memory is fickle and unreliable, meaning that we can never arrive at a point of so-called conclusion full of confidence that what we have achieved along the way of our memorializing and culturally investigative meanderings, our psycho-social perambulations, is a clear and accurate picture of who we are; that what we have at hand, instead of an authoritative account of our creative disposition, is nothing more than a version, an imagining and a possibility of this character that is no more or no less valid than any number of alternative results that we might achieve, on another day, under different emotional or inter-personal circumstances. Does this mean that what I am evidently invested in is nothing more than a futile process doomed to failure because it doesn't actually anchor in reality. Does it mean that I'm not remembering but rather making stuff up, being creative with my own personal history, thus with my trajectory? Could I be, somewhere along the lines that I attempt to trace, somehow lying to myself even unwittingly, innocently, because I want to be better, because I care too much about advancing my creative capacities, and entertaining myself, spending time, formulating patterns from which I might ascertain something interesting enough to deem worthy of creative application? I'm not really convinced that what I am doing has a rational basis and yet I keep going as if it were all comprehensive. I wonder, what is wrong with what I already have, with what I already understand, that I should seek so enthusiastically for something more than it is? What is lacking or missing with regard to the present state of my creative practice that I should choose to deconstruct it in this way. What is the basis of my incredulity? It cannot be profound disadvantage. After all, I am not disabled, not without a comfortable home or without ready access to various creative tools, with which I may make music whenever I want. I can spend time jumping around in circles on the trampoline with my daughter, while holding her hands making up ridiculous songs that make us laugh and fall about. I have a loving partner. The world is filled with things so much more important than what I might call my art. Is taking the heavy-handed approach to a light task, thus opting to invest far more time than is recommended, too indulgent? How can I put this into words? Why should I?

Memory is fickle and unreliable, and not much helped by language. This is a fairly well-established consideration made when making sense of the veracity and limitation of any creative activity, dating all the way back almost two-and-a-half thousand years to where we find Plato's view of artistic activity. Plato (427–347 BC) is an important figure for making even the most cursory of art-historical references because our contemporary Western philosophical ideas, having emanated from the earliest Western civilizations such as Greece, are grounded in Platonic thinking. Plato's influence on the arts is broad reaching, even though not all of it was positive. He valued logical thought above emotional or irrational thought, and thought that artists, such as the playwright Homer, were guilty of this so-called weakness.

Plato's masterpiece, the *Republic*, is a Socratic dialogue written in ten books, the whole of which provides the reader with a representation of Socrates, of how he talked, of his teaching, but above all an insight into the proposed meaningfulness of his life. Plato's *Republic* lays out his imagining of the composition of an ideal society. This is a society in which he denigrates the status of artists; they are deemed to not have a valuable function in a society where logic attracts the highest value. Of course, this value judgement will only ring true if, at the back of it all, there exists a very particular assumption about the nature and function of art as a form of productivity that is biased towards the irrational, the non-linear, the counter-logical, the intuitive, the tacit, and that which embraces the logic of improvisation in a spirit of adventure—traits that align closely with how Ulmer would like us to approach a mystoriographical experiment. Through Plato's ideological lens, it could be said, art has little to no capacity to make an important or lasting contribution to the society in which it has been produced. This is despite art being, to take a social constructionist point of view that enables us to switch around cause and effect, a product of its socio-cultural environment; society has provided the material and infrastructural nourishment from which creative acts feed, even implicitly, for no art exists in isolation, in a vacuum. In other words, society causes the art of its time to happen, with the result being that art provides a mirror for its reflection. A society that denigrates creative reflection is a poor one and thus, from my perspective, not ideal at all.

This is a bigger issue that has been sufficiently addressed and that, in any case, might distract us from the path we are presently on — one that leads us to Book 7 of Plato's *Republic* (set between 443–404 BCE and written about 380 BCE), and perhaps the most famous image in the Western historical tradition of art. This image is commonly known as the *allegory of the cave*, and is a meditation on the relationship between the realm of *ideas* and the realm of *appearances*, which we can refer to as *theory* and *practice.*

Plato, who was influenced by the ideas of Parmenides (c. 515–450 B.C.) was the first philosopher to document his reflections on the subject of ideal forms. Since the world of experience is illusory only the eternal is real, so Plato speculated, in this realm eternal, unchanging forms exist. They are the blueprints or the universal forms. According to Plato, there are many individual dogs, horses and cats, but they are all made in the image of the one universal form of a dog, a cat, or horse, which, in this way, presents a kind of proto-semiotics. The corruption of art, it would seem, resides in its incapacity to achieve more than imperfect copies of worldly copies of the ideal forms, his aspatial and atemporal blue-prints for all matter in the universe, existing in a transcendental realm beyond the entropic, spatiality, and temporality of the physical world. The allegory of the cave articulates Plato's exploration of the extent to which human nature is enlightened or unenlightened. To explain, inside the cave, slaves are chained in such a way that they can only face the wall. They are presented as having always been this way; the interior of the cave is the only world they know. Also in the cave, located behind the slaves, a fire is burning brightly, and between the slaves and the fire there is a walkway. People are crossing this walkway on their way to the marketplace, carrying out their daily affairs with their goods and animals, and are talking amongst themselves. Due to their physical constraints, the slaves cannot turn around to see the passers-by. All they can see, all they have ever seen, are the distorted shadows of the figures that are cast onto the cave wall by the light of the fire. All they can hear are the voices of the shadows, their constituent sonic frequencies bouncing around the walls of the cave uncontrollably, which reach the ears of the slaves as nothing more than waves of muffled incoherence. The slaves are blissfully ignorant that anything exists outside the shadows, lacking any knowledge that an outside (real) world even exists.

One day, a guard releases the chains of one of the prisoners, the ancient Greek word for which is *Lysius* [Λύω (lou)]—to loosen/unbind, the surname of Dionysus, the deliverer, indicating that the slave is on his way to freedom. In effect, by being set free, the slave is now required to turn around and examine his life, recalling Socrates's belief that "life without this sort of examination is not worth living" (Plato 72). An element of educational violence can be detected here (also present in another dialogue written by Plato called *Meno*), though certainly not one that would be acceptable in our own ethically aware, contemporary pedagogical institutions.

The slave's release from the cave is rendered as a natural process, in turn rendering confinement in the cave as unnatural, which perhaps explains why the prisoner's release is sometimes interpreted as him being dragged out of the cave. After this release/dragging, the now-free individual draws closer and closer to the outside world, approaching exteriority, seeing first the fire, the puppeteers, and then the cave mouth, before stepping up to experience the light of the sun.

At first, the slave's eyes can't adjust to the light, so he starts out by looking at the reflections he notices in the water, and in the night sky. Once his eyes have adjusted, he is able to see all of the things that had been crossing the walkway and which, before now, he had only comprehended in shadowy form. He sees the world for what it is, and with this moment of illumination and enlightenment, he feels the desire to return to the cave so that he can share with everybody his new-found knowledge of the remarkable things that he has discovered. At this point in the narrative, we can see how the prisoner has started out in a passive role, yet by the end of the story, through learning about the world, we can see that he has evolved into an active participant. Herein lies a lesson in the responsibility that stems from education—the responsibility of sharing knowledge (or not being jealous when it comes to ideas), along with all the inefficiencies of pedagogical transmission, as challenges to be met, that this form of scholarship might bring; I am using the word *scholarship* in cognizance of Ernest Boyer's model of the style of learning that is brought back into the classroom for shared, educational benefit. Here, scholarship can refer to activities that an educator engages in either individually or collaboratively to inform and improve "student learning in a specific course or discipline" (Trigwell et al., 165). This, to reflect on Plato's cave, translates to a conscientious attempt to share access to freedom; learning is a liberatory practice. The kind of learning that is brought to bear through a mystoriograhical narrative might be less to do with self-indulgence (connoting an active entrenchment in the self) than it is to do with a freedom and autonomy from the self—a quasi-Nietzschean overcoming, and mastery, of the self through vigorous self-education, an aggressive project of evolution.

> Behold, I teach you the overman. Man is something that shall be overcome. What have you done to overcome him? All beings so far have created something beyond themselves; and do you want to be the ebb of this great flood and even go back to the beasts rather than overcome man? What is the ape to man? A laughingstock or a painful embarrassment. And man shall be just that for the overman: a laughingstock or a painful embarrassment . . . The overman is the meaning of the earth. . . . *remain faithful to the earth* . . . (Nietzsche "Thus Spoke Zarathustra: A Book for All and None" 124–25)

One of the lesson's of Plato's cave is that education brings with it responsibility, specifically the social responsibility that one has to share their knowledge with generosity. While the ideal is admirable, Plato's allegory warns us that this practice is not without risk of hindrance, risk of retaliation from one's community, risk of ridicule, and that this risk might even be a logical outcome of one's efforts to articulate personal evolution. In Plato's allegory, when the now-free individual (no longer a slave to their conditioning, but mobilized within it) returns to the cave, he calls out to the slaves still facing the wall. Yet, his words reverberate uncontrollably around the interior space so that they reach the ears of the slaves as muffled incoherence. The now-free individual waves his arms about in an attempt to attract their attention, yet, just like the passers-by and their animals before, this time too, the light of the fire interferes, casting his distorted shadow on the cave wall. The free individual realizes

> that the prisoners cannot recognise their own friend. He appears as all things do—his voice is a distorted echo and his body is a grotesque shadow. They cannot understand his fantastic stories of the world outside of the cave. To them, it will

> never exist. This, of course, does not make the world outside of the cave any less real. (Ramsey)

Plato's allegory of the cave gives us a veritable ancient cinema that functions as an allegory of the life of Socrates himself, who tried to convince the bewitched prisoners of the mind that *the truth is out there*, a trope we see employed in a range of media productions, particularly the *X-Files* television series, but also in *The Matrix* movie trilogy and the film *The Truman Show*—both contemporary renditions of Plato's cave allegory, encouraging us to defamiliarize our habituated ways of seeing and understanding the world around us and the events that take place in it, so as to evolve our comprehension and, thus, our capacity to creatively communicate with each other about the issues and ideas we find important, so as to remain constructively critical when encountering versions of truth portrayed by people in positions of power, for example. As Giddens says, "[p]owerful groups are able to control the dominant ideas circulating in a society so as to justify their own position" (*Sociology* 381). Plato's allegory, plus the contemporary renditions acknowledged above, are politically loaded narratives; they are all relatable to the contexts of power in which individual lives go on. To this extent, each instance presents the viewer with a model for thinking imaginatively about what it might mean to live an authentic life (i.e., in an honest, authoritative, and empowered way).

If Plato's cave can be interpreted as an ancient cinema, it is not surprising, then, that we may come to re-imagine the *shadows* on the walls as *representations* analogous to those displayed on the walls of cultural institutions (art galleries and museums, for the purposes of either private or public display). Art, in this sense, presents as a signifier of shadows and/or versions of the world that we might do best to approach with healthy incredulity. This is reflected in work by the ancient Greek philosopher Aristotle, a student of Plato who also meditated on the nature of art, echoing his mentor's thought in understanding that art is merely an imitation of reality; a mirror held up to nature, for sure, but never nature itself, always detached from it (Poetics 1447). Many philosophers since Aristotle have agreed with this view. In the words of German philosopher Friedrich Nietzsche, "[a]rt, in the narrow sense, is yes-saying to the sensuous, to semblance, to what is not 'the true world,' or as [he] says succinctly, to what is not 'the truth.' . . . [a]rt is worth more than the truth," taken here as the demonstration of metaphysical will (qtd. in Heidegger 74–75).

For Nietzsche, "[w]e have art in order not to perish from the truth" (qtd. in Heidegger 75). It is a thought well worth keeping in mind for someone embarking upon an experiment in mystoriography. This is optional, of course; one needn't get too caught up in the philosophical thinking of the distant past when there is enough contemporary discourse reiterating, through explication and exploitation of, the slipperiness of the language with which we try to weight things down in the world, vainly attempting to secure them with the anchors of symbolism and signification—the very language, "a new form of writing," through which a mystory find its articulation (Hawk 238). "Die Grenzen meiner Sprache bedeuten die Grenzen meiner Welt [The limits of my language mean the limits of my world]," wrote Austrian philosopher Ludwig Wittgenstein in the only book he published in his lifetime, *Tractatus Logico-Philosophicus* (5.6). Today, this sentiment adds to our post-structuralist, post-modern, playful dubiety as to the capacity of language to articulate whatever half-truths of our shared or personal pasts our fallible memory manages to muster, reminding us that we are trapped within the doubly problematic and parallaxical circumstance of a mystoriographical investigation. An understanding of this scene of language-play can benefit from Dick Hebdige's discussion on subcultures and style, throughout which he applies the semiotic analytical techniques that are often traced back to French theorist Roland Barthes. Hebdige asks what is signified by subcultural style, taking the language, visuality, and sonics of British punk culture of the 1970s as his case study—the multi-modal text to be culturally read. Yet, along the way towards answering his question, Hebdige needs to acknowledge some of the conditions of language that reflect our current landscape and which, therefore, add useful insight into the ground-works for a particular project.

Raising language's inability to draw us to a conclusive set of meanings, and to traditional semiotics's response, Hebdige (117–18) says that:

> the simple notion of reading as the revelation of a fixed number of concealed meanings is discarded in favour of the idea of *polysemy* whereby each text is seen to generate a potentially infinite range of meanings. Attention is consequently directed towards that point—or more precisely, that level—in any given text where the principle of meaning itself seems most in doubt. Such an approach lays less stress on the primacy of

> structure and system in language ("langue"), and more upon the *position* of the speaking subject in discourse ("parole"). It is concerned with the process of meaning construction rather than the product.

The use-value of Hebdige's insight is as follows: given the broader definitions of a *text* as anything that can be *culturally read*, as an object ever available as the direct object of critical analysis (albeit often approached in a seemingly indirect way), the personal and cultural histories stored in our memories are texts and, thus, subjected to the same limitations and vulnerabilities as other forms of text—in addition to the memory issue previously stated (double parallax). The semiotic context echoes the neuro-scientific context in its denial of the singularity and stability of meaning. For the mystoriographical project, this means (*among other possibilities of equal legitimacy*) that loci of doubt are not problematic in the way that a cul-de-sac might seem to hinder the pathway. Rather, they motivate the investigative mood in which meaningfulness, joy, in the hypothetical hunt can be derived. Just as the writing of W. G. Sebald is so often punctuated by doubt, so too does it seem pertinent to rest awhile on those moments and happenings, in a mystoriography, that we likewise might have encountered " . . . for reasons which were never entirely clear to me" (*Austerlitz* 1).

In addition, Hebdige cites a concern with the position of the speaker; is it already clear that the creative exhumation of disposition comprises the central motivation of mystoriographical work. This tactical linkage to semiotic theory helps us to see part of the established research to which a mystory, as an example of language-bound work, continuously speaks. The mystory, to borrow a concept largely associated with the *Tel Quel* group, is therefore perhaps best thought of as a *signifying practice.* This concept of the signifying practice reflected the Tel Quel group's

> central concerns with the ideological implications of form, with the idea of a positive construction and deconstruction of meaning, and with what has come to be called the "productivity" of language. This approach sees language as an active, transitive force which shapes and positions the subject (as speaker, writer, reader) while always itself remaining "in process" capable of infinite adaptation. This emphasis on signifying practice is accompanied by a polemical insistence that

> art represents the triumph of process over fixity, disruption over unity, "collision" over "linkage"—the triumph, that is, of the signifier over the signified. It should be seen as part of the group's attempt to substitute the values of 'fissure' and contradiction for the preoccupation with "wholeness" [i.e., the text conceived as a closed structure (Lackner and Matias, 1972)] which is said to characterize classic literary criticism. (Hebdige 119)

Mystoriographical work takes place in the post-traditional context, actively shaping cultural, self-comprehension through the production of a critical auto-ethnographic dialogue that appeals to a sense of authenticity, if only by being transparent about the inherent opacity and entropy of its own communicative conditions.

There is no truth to be found here, none convincingly ahead, suggesting a form of fate with which heed need be taken, a certain resignation. Perhaps what is to be found is better in some way, better than truth, better than certitude, as if language consoles us for the past that it ultimately denies by giving us permission to make revisions, adaptations, acclimatizing us to the past in some way so to ignite its relevance to the present—yes-saying to the life-affirming presence of history. It may strike us as necessary that a plurality of attempts be made, so that each on its own can be examined and triangulated with, mapped against, alternative attempts in the group, yet, still, all we would perhaps be left with is a mapping of artifice, conceptual errors of growing complexity, no closer to the certainty that our human condition relentlessly denies us. We might resemble laborers conducting an archaeological dig for hidden traces and treasures, spellbound by nocturnal aspiration—diggers in the dark, or else some other species of geographically displaced and dis-positioned angler fish, our working area illuminated by head-torch lumens, on a treasure hunt for memories (like the mineral samples of our distant pasts that, in my case, and according to the geological accounts I have read, would include globules of pearlescent sky blue allophane found on slate matrix, Pale buff colored columnar masses embedded in dense, dark, gray, and finely grained matrices of manganese oxides, blister copper, brown Childrenite crystals and micro green Arthurite coatings). These are memories that, even under the most ideal of meteorological conditions, might never quite satisfy the human eye, that physiological referent for the guiding light of the enlightenment, the empirical method. What we have here is more intimate, less tangible; what we are dealing with is the mind's eye, and what the mystory might move to exhume from within it, as recollections, as freely re-emerging memory work, or some kind of self-creative psychotherapy, a private speech under ongoing transcription. "When memories come back to you, you sometimes feel as if you were looking at the past through a glass mountain" (Sebald *Austerlitz* 224). When I think about these words, in this order (co-incidentally, while listening to Philip Glass's *Glassworks* from 1982), an image of the human condition comes to mind wherein we catch a glimpse of something beyond us, clearly seeing what we will never touch again, misting up the nonporous and impenetrable façade with warm breath and maybe leaving a nose smudge or lip marks, when we recede back into forgetting.

It is as if we can hope to become, only, increasingly adept at affecting the process, growing muscle in some Sisyphean task, and so we conclude, as did Camus at the end of his analysis of this ancient Greek myth, where we find Sisyphus, the protagonist, no higher in altitude than the day he received his sentence of eternal bondage. His task, too, seems absurd, and being committed to it might lead the passer-by to suspect he is bound not to a task imposed upon him but, rather, to a pleasure-bringing madness of his own making.

> The rock is still rolling. I leave Sisyphus at the foot of the mountain! One always finds one's burden again. But Sisyphus teaches the higher fidelity that negates the gods and raises rocks. He too concludes that all is well. This universe henceforth without a master seems to him neither sterile nor futile. Each atom of that stone, each mineral flake of that night-filled mountain, in itself forms a world. The struggle itself toward the heights is enough to fill a man's heart. One must imagine Sisyphus happy. (Camus 123)

Perhaps we are all, always already, tied by our language dependency and by our neurological constitution, at the base of the mountain. For the mystory, it can be said that Ulmer never expects to uncover an unassailable truth and refrains from deflecting this expectation onto individuals who have set out on a mystoriographical journey. Instead, through adopting mystoriography as a form of art practice (in which we have seen to be embedded its own notes of absurdity), continuing the Socratic method of continual undermining, we have at our disposal a means by which to generate our own sense of mastery in the world. By embracing the absurdity of the process (as a metonym for the absurdity of our human condition), we can focus on the activities that exercise meaning-making, purpose-building, and that may even lead us to happiness.

This happiness can at least in part be experienced as the pleasure derived from actively and self-consciously reading and decoding the semiotic content of the texts of our cultural histories. What emerges, through such analysis, is an improvised literary identity, presented in the form of a hypothesis that may be amended or appended as new insight comes to hand, and one that can perhaps also be understood as the pleasurable exploration of our own *cultural capital*—a concept attributed to Pierre Bourdieu, described by Peter Brooker as

> the possession of knowledge, accomplishments, formal and informal qualifications by which an individual may gain entry and secure a position in particular social circles, professions and organizations. It may therefore be seen as a more systematic way of accounting for what is entailed in loose descriptions of the 'cultured' individual or social type [disposition]. (54)

If the mystory is defined by flux, by insecurity, by parallax, not only because of the mode of articulation I have chosen for its exposition (writing), but because I am attempting to explain it at all, then it is absurd. But truth is not the highest goal, and we need not wander down the road to anhedonia just because what we are dealing with defies the comforting embrace of resolution and self-affirmation; perhaps these things will come to us in the end, but they need not be all that keeps us going, not all that feeds creative evolution, that feeds the impulse to make a cultural contribution. For me, embarking on a mystory, on this experimental research process, most of all means accepting the responsibility for my own esthetic direction, of my own expertise, of my own purpose. I begin this with the understanding that the mystory is an opportunity for me to demonstrate, for myself and maybe for others, independence and resilience when it comes to the task of driving my own creative development forward, whatever the speed the images flash past my mind's eye, as if in a speeding car, during a quick footed dérive through the city's streets or, as it comes to me now, like the kind of stroboscopic hallucination Brion Gysin's famous *Dream Machine* might induce and which, now that I've mentioned it, warrants some degree of explanation.

The cognitive effects of light flickering in the retinal field were first described by Jan E. Purkinje in 1823 but were later re-visited by Brion Gysin and Ian Sommerville following Gysin's journey from Paris to the Mediterranean artist's colony *La Ciotat* on December 21, 1958.

> As the bus passed through a long avenue of trees Gysin, closing his eyes against the setting sun, encountered "a transcendental storm of color visions. . . . [a]n overwhelming flood of intensely bright patterns in supernatural colors exploded behind my eyelids: a multidimensional kaleidoscope whirling through space. I was swept out of time." (Geiger 11)

Flickering light has been used in many films to signify an impending blackout, as an ominous symbol of the end of knowledge or the onset of vulnerability in the face of the *unknown*. But it was a result of Gysin's experience that him and Sommerville started working on a machine that would allow users, as producers and not simply consumers of the visual experience, to control when, where, and for how long such a hallucination would occur, leading them to perhaps use the insight gained from this experience in their subsequent creative works. The invention can be readily reproduced today, and for very little cost. To make one of your own (first ensuring that you do not have a family history of photosensitive epilepsy), take a rectangular piece of card and cut a repeated pattern into it (there are various patterns available online that one may choose from). Then, roll the modified card into a cylinder and place it upright on a record player turntable. There should be no light in the room, except for a single light bulb that has been lowered inside the cylinder. Sit close to it and set the turntable to spin. Close your eyes. Relax. Wait.

As the cut-outs moves past the visual field, a flickering effect is produced on the user's eyelids that over-stimulates the optic nerve. Whether out of some fight or flight response (a human need to make sense of the visual chaos in the absence of any external reference), the idea is that the user is forced to draw on the vast stock of images held in the recesses of their mind. William Burroughs and Peggy Guggenheim experienced hallucinations, as did prospective patron Helena Rubenstein, to whom the visions appeared "like films" (Geiger 64). In the context of Cold War politics, at the onset of the Vietnam War, and on the eve of American counter-cultural/sub-cultural movements such as the Beatnik generation and then the hippies, the Dream Machine attracted much attention. Some of this was positive; the artistic community had taken it as an exciting new tool for generating creative awareness, a mechanical and drug-free alternative to prohibited substances such as MDMA, Ecstasy, Psilocybin, and LSD (though it was sometimes used in conjunction with these drugs)—a machine powerful enough to produce hallucinations and yet controllable enough that these hallucinations would cease without side-effects the moment the cylinder stopped spinning. It still does: "[i]n 2000, Gysin and Somerville's invention was included in an exhibition of art concerned with dreams and altered states of consciousness titled *Dream Machine*, organized by the Hayward Gallery, London, and selected by Susan Hiller, an American artist living in Britain" (Geiger 97). Gysin "had provided others with an outlet, a means of accessing something, of introducing illumination at the flick of a switch, a means to 'get a voyage underway,' a means of discovery" (Geiger 99). In an article co-authored with Michael Mason, which contained "the first serious attempt, other than its inventors, to explain the Dream Machine to a broader public," author Richard Condon wrote that the Dream Machine provokes

> something a little fancier than dreaming and a little less fancy than the recovery of pre-experiential memory. . . . The Dream Machine rearranges components of experience into patterns which are new even to the unconscious mind and they do this by presenting to the perceptual system inputs of such extraordinary novelty that the mind/memory system hauls out is entire stock of perception memories and concept-memories and works itself dizzy trying to assemble and test different combinations of these components in an effort to recognize or explain the totally new perceptions . . . The Dream Machine presents an oscillation between consciousness and memory. (qtd. in Geiger 78–9)

It was while reflecting on his experience during a 1962 demonstration of one of Gysin's flickering creations, that the English writer Norman Lewis Glass acknowledged, "only by man's jump into the unknown will he arrive to understand and manage the known" (Geiger 62). For Jean Fischer, Gysin's dream machine existed in close proximity to syncope; "a momentary loss of breath, a blackout, an ecstatic insight, eclipse of thought, an off-beat that introduces dissonance into a rhythmic flow," in which, in Geiger's (102) view, "time is suspended." For the French philosopher Catherine Clémen, flicker's syncopated dimension resonates with the physical disturbances caused by an epileptic fit, which she termed "an apparent death" (qtd. in Geiger 102). For an individual, in the wake of their seizure, "it is the real world that suddenly looks strange" (Geiger 103).

I do not wish, at this point, to delve too deeply into the location of the Dream Machine in the greater history of stroboscopics. Nevertheless, it is interesting to note the theoretical ambitions it shares with mystoriographical activity. My engagement in a veritable dérive through some of the theoretical tendrils of the process to come has led me to thinking about the role of flicker in human sensory perception and about how this might be applied in creative non-fiction such as this. As Michael Hutchison says, "[t]he knowledge that a flickering light can cause visual hallucinations is something humans have known since the discovery of fire," and I also remain well aware of this fact (Geiger 11). Here, however, in the context of preparing the stage for a mystoriograhical journey, my thinking around the usefulness of the Dream Machine as a model of thinking extends. It speaks to the bubbling up of the past, it speaks to velocity, it speaks to the personal-metaphysical, the experimental, the peripheral, the transgressive (in terms of troubling an existing state of play through conscientious and prolonged interrogation), to the defamiliarization of a creative trajectory and, thus, the underlying disposition that may have been taken for granted, as given, but now to see it as in flux, negotiable, not inevitable, vulnerable to change, to disturbance, to improvement; to see it new again as if with the eyes of a curious alien (an alien susceptible to cognitive dis-inhibition. It provides a suitable metaphor by which we can further understand for the present experimental, investigative mood.

"Your creativity starts with whether you're curious or not," says architect Frank Gehry (Master Class). I agree, and expect that this is why the mystory appeals to me so much. For, whatever disposition it might prove to uncover, whatever other gains can be anticipated in return for the effort made, the mystory is first and foremost about engaging curiosity, providing an investigative structure suitable to its negotiation and transmutation. Curiosity keeps us wondering, wandering, and makes us available for learning; it is one of the core values that will keep us moving forward—into the unknown, with an open mind.

2 Mystory: Creative Cultural Practice

More broadly, mystoriography can be defined as an attempt to conduct and represent research in terms of three general domains of discourse: the professional (any branch of formal knowledge or expertise); the popular (including both contemporary pop culture forms, such as music or television, and more traditional resources, such as family lore, community stories, oral histories, etc.); and the personal (individual memories, experiences). In short, the mystory assumes that identity is enciphered by means of certain dominant institutional discourses. Researching and writing one's mystory is thus an attempt to decipher one's identity by tracking down and interrogating specific texts from these discourses."

— Nathan Stucky, Cynthia Wimmer, and Richard Schechner

The various reference points that have been presented so far form a map that leads us to the following place of understanding—to the importance of thinking critically about our creative acts, our representations shared in the world that, as the French theorist Christian Metz proposed, "are all fictional . . . since they all re-present something by means of signs, rather than by presenting what exists in the spectator's real time and space" (Bignell 184). Metz was focusing on cinema and identified three processes in cinema spectatorship, which "were identification, voyeurism and fetishism involving disavowal of lack" (Bignell 184). As Jonathan Bignell says: "[t]he ability of the technical apparatus of cinema to make an absence present is one form of fetishism, and representations which themselves cover but reveal lack and absence are fetishistic too" (186). Bignell's insight is relevant to the theoretical considerations and questions that have been raised, due to the analogical relationship that cinema has to the broader game of representation, performed on the basis of memory (as a form of imaginative cinema). The mystory, it can be said, finds us entering into this representation of absences, in the imaginative production of fetishistic elements, making present, in altered states, the experiences of our pasts, observations made in the skillfully controlled, ambient light of tele-visual media and, to a not insignificant degree, observations on the cultural circumstances in which we believe these recollections and observations take place.

Taking the time to consider the theoretical backdrop to a creative activity like the mystory is important, as it is in the context of any creative activity. This importance has been recognized since the last days of Socrates, encapsulated in the sentiment that theory without practice is poor and practice without theory is also poor. When and where theory and practice are separate (estranged, without communication), we may describe this distance, this space of disconnection, as a site of impoverishment. It is not, however, an impoverishment that is distant from us, in our acts, but one that may become our impoverishment (one under which we might continue to work, perhaps unwittingly), that we can embrace. Offering a theoretical structure, therefore, is to provide a framework around which a practice may then be arranged, hung. Ironically, the theory presented makes for a vertiginous sight with which I am faced as I shift now into the practice of the mystory, not wholly forthcoming in the stability and reassurance that we might expect of a scaffolding made of steel that enables safe restoration work on the façade of an existing building, for example. Instead, the step into practice is made under conditions of verifiable insecurity and instability, doubt in the veracity of the human memory that, thus, pushes towards the imaginative. This does not mean we should denounce authenticity.

Ulmer's notion of the mystory, insight into a person's disposition, is affected through an analysis of three discrete realms of experience. As Ulmer says:

> Write a mystory bringing into relation your experience with three levels of discourse—personal (autobiography), popular (community stories, oral history or popular culture), expert (disciplines of knowledge). In each case use the *punctum* or sting of memory to locate items significant to you; once located, research

> the representations of the popular and expert items [pertaining to the community or discipline in which one becomes an expert/professional] in the archive or encyclopaedia (thus mixing living and artificial memories). (*Teletheory* 209)

Once these three domains of, what Ulmer calls, a *popcycle* have been imagined, outlined, and researched, a pattern across them is ascertained by way of one's answering three questions:

> 1. How does the world work? What is reality? What does the mystoriography tell me about the answer to this question?
>
> 2. Consult the mystoriographical pattern to answer the question "what is your morality?" How should I behave in light of this apparent world-working?
>
> 3. How do I feel about it? What is the mood in which I undertake these actions in the world (i.e., the attitude, the aesthetic? [qtd. in Vardouli, "Gregory L. Ulmer on Mystoriography (Teletheory, 1989)"]

It is important to note that one stage of the mystory is used to answer one question. This said, and as far as Ulmer is concerned, it doesn't matter which question is answered by which stage. I will refrain from pairing discourse levels with questions until all three stages have been completed.

1. Other People's Stories

Memory work is done to bring strong images of childhood experience to the surface. In his MIT lecture, Ulmer uses the example of Maurice Sendak's memory of a hardcover cloth-bound book that his sister received in the mail (she belonged to a book club) [Vardouli, "Gregory L. Ulmer on Mystoriography (Teletheory, 1989)"]. It was the biggest, greenest book Maurice had ever seen, and he became obsessed with it, even though he was not yet able to read. Sendak became so obsessed, in fact, that his mother ended up convincing Maurice's sister to give him the book just to restore some peace. Sendak loved the book so much that (despite being unable to read, or perhaps even because of it) he licked the book all over until eventually he ruined it. When he eventually found himself in possession of a soggy, saliva-damaged artifact, Sendak lost interest and gave it back to his sister. There is a clear fetishistic aspect here, in the repeated oral contact with and literal wettening of literature. Ulmer presents this physicality as insight into the early childhood love of books felt by a young person whose rich literary career as the author and illustrator of dozens of books was yet to unfold. Thinking about the symbolic meaning of licking, I am reminded of the sexual symbolism found in Greek artifacts, such as that found

> [o]n the Greek medals, where the cow is the symbol of the deity, she is frequently represented licking a calf, which is suckling her. This is probably meant to show that the creative power cherishes and nourishes, as well as generates; for, as all quadrupeds lick their young, to refresh and invigorate them immediately after birth, it is natural to suppose, according to the general system of symbolic writing, that this action should be taken as an emblem of the effect it was thought to produce. (Knight and Wright 48)

With this additional information, we can recognize Sendak's gesture as fetishistic in general, for he imbues the book with a symbolic power that far exceeds its materiality; specifically, this can be described as the book's power to provide Sendak with creative energy and capacity in life.

Ulmer also shares the story of one of the most important architects of the late modern age, Frank Gehry (1929-), the Canadian born innovator described by Vanity Fair as "the most important architect of our age" (Tyrnauer). Gehry has designed numerous well-known buildings in the deconstructivist style including the *Vitra Design Museum* (Weil am Rhein, Germany, completed 1989), the *Dancing House* (Prague, completed 1996) and the *Walt Disney Concert Hall* (Los Angeles, completed 2003), *8 Spruce Street* (New York, completed 2010), and many more that incorporate complex shapes and angles, using technology to explore the limits of constructability. This esthetic is evident in examples of Gehry's architectural work such as the geometrically complex, *Guggenheim Museum* located in Bilbao, Spain, its façade clad with 42,875 titanium panels, a low-density, high-strength material not often used in building (Mendelsohn). Its visual appearance has been likened to crinkled cardboard or a scrunched up ball of paper, though the oscillating locomotion of a goldfish's fins provide a rather more poetic point of reference. It is one of the reasons why Ulmer, in his MIT lecture, cites Gehry's childhood fascination with the style of motion displayed by his pet goldfish (and not simply because Ulmer's addressing an audience comprising architecture students) as key to the idiosyncratic buildings that have brought Gehry so much adulation and criticism [Vardouli, "Gregory L. Ulmer on Mystoriography (Teletheory, 1989)"].

I would like to add two further examples to the current pool, however incomplete, of dispositional souvenirs. The first of these is the contemporary American artist Bill Viola who has worked extensively in the field of video installation. Viola is an internationally respected artist with many of his works concentrating on the human body as a vehicle for the expression of physical experience, as opposed to intellectual experience. Shown at the *Exposition au Grand Palais*, Paris in 2014, Viola's work *The Dreamers* (2013) is an example of his attention to detail achieved through the use of extreme slow motion. In this work, we find an extension of Viola's investigation into our relationship to water. This artwork comprises seven individual screens, each of which is sixty-five inches in size and vertically mounted in a darkened room measuring 6.5 meters (length) x 6.5 meters (width) x 3.5 meters (height). They display slow motion footage of people who look as though they are sleeping underwater as their breath causes bubbles to form that float to the surface, offering the viewer rare instances of movement. Viola is known for creating video works that immerse the viewer's senses; in the darkened installation environment, the large-scale images are accompanied by the sounds of the water. The intention is to draw the viewer into the work, in this way making them feel as if they were also submerged under water.

For this discussion, the interest-value of *The Dreamers* artwork exists beyond the heavily coded museum context—instead situated in the intimate, interior space of childhood memory. This becomes clear to us in a Bill Viola interview, during which Viola shares a childhood memory. He explains how, at the age of six, he nearly drowned in a lake north of New York. He was jumping off of a pontoon with his cousin, even though he was unable to swim. Viola describes the event:

> I got in my little inner tube; I jumped off and I didn't realise that you were supposed to hold onto it, so I just went right to the bottom like a stone. I open my eyes and I saw the most beautiful world I've ever seen, shafts of light coming down, gorgeous. There were plants moving on the bottom in a beautiful way. Everything was blue and green, and I just sat down like a little Buddha, right on the bottom, and I just looked around at this world, and it was the most beautiful thing I'd ever seen. (Blain Southern)

In this interview, Viola talks about having seen a big hand coming down and pulling him out, his uncle's hand saving him from death, and seeing his mother crying. What's interesting here, so far as it pertains to this mystoriographical project, is Viola's admission that he'd never thought about the significance of this experience until an interview that he'd had in his twenties when, having mentioned the near-drowning experience to the interviewer, having added it almost as a passing detail with no inkling of it being a significant event with future artistic implications, the interviewer said: "Oh, that's why you use so much water in your work." As Viola says, "That's when I realised that water is everything for me. It's what I do" (Blain Southern).

Although Viola goes on to talk about the role of water in Palaeolithic times as the natural mirror into which human beings first got to experience their reflection, listening to him speak, my mental focus remained fixed on this discovered connection between Viola's family memory and his creative disposition. However, it is not so much the fact that a connection exists, but that this connection seems to have gone unnoticed over a long period of time, permeating his arts practice on a subconscious level; the *discovery*, albeit made by the interviewing third party, presents to us a return of the repressed. This exhumation of hidden meaning is arresting, in part at least, because the interviewer from long ago caught sight of the foundations of a major aspect of Viola's work before he did. This modality of outsidership, of critical distance, is perhaps another manifestation of cognitive parallax, as aforementioned in this mystoriographical narrative; it is as if the interviewer, having metaphorically peered over Viola's shoulder like the passenger in a motor vehicle, glimpsed momentarily, and from an angle, the speedometer located directly in front of the driver (what was staring Viola in the face, that he may well have looked at, mechanically, but which he had not yet noticed emotionally, intellectually, dispositionally). The observing subject (the interviewer) sat adjacent to the direct object (Viola, as interviewee), gaining insight from this circumferential position that, as it came to pass, catalysed gainful communication around what, using Ulmer's phraseology, we might call Viola's invariant principle.

Born in 1951, Bill Viola was already in his early thirties before he realized the impact that his childhood near-death experience had on his creative work (that crucial interview having taken place circa the mid-eighties). It was not a fleeting fancy, brought up in a controlled environment only to be forgotten again once the cameras had cut. For thirty years later, Viola still regards his near-death story as a cornerstone to his creative identity. In the interview titled *Bill Viola: Cameras are the Keepers of the Soul*, conducted by Christian Lund in London, 2011, and produced by the Louisiana Museum of Modern Art, Viola talks again about his childhood, about how he spent it as a shy and introverted person. He talks about his studio as being the center of his work and, to this extent, the nerve center and command post of his creative world, and about having used notebooks as a means of maintaining a constant dialogue with himself since he was about twelve years old. Then Lund, the interviewer asks Viola: "When did you find out that images played an important role in your life?" Viola recounts the near-death story, adding:

> I see it regularly; I see it constantly almost in my mind and my mind's eye. . . . I just felt that was the real world [the world at the bottom of the lake]. I was very lucky 'cos I didn't die. My uncle saved me. But what happened was I was shown, just by this accident, that there's more than just the surface of life, you know, that the real thing is under the surface. (Louisiana Museum of Modern Art)

This sense of what was *real*, not the truth of reality but, rather, something that Viola was able to tip into another reality, into art, was better than truth (i.e., a sense of sites unseen beneath the visible, the surreptitious, tides undetected that, nevertheless, move us this way and that).

Given the vast amount of biological, spiritual, technological, emotional, and intellectual information to which Viola was exposed in the quarter of a century between the time of his near-drowning and the moment of his mid-interview self-realization, it is no wonder that he had almost forgotten about it until then. It is no wonder that it took another person's parallaxical insight to bring this vital connection to Viola's attention. I wonder, as a member of Viola's art-viewing audience, whether we even need Viola's confirmation to comprehend the basis of his work. Consider the darkened room installation called *Five angels for the Millenium* (2001), a video comprised of five projections in full color with stereo audio, and in each of them a clothed male can be seen rising and descending into a pool of water, his movements shown in slow motion. Alternatively, Viola's slow motion video *The Raft* (2004), displays a group of clothed people standing together, a torrent of water crashing into them from the viewer's left hand side and saturating them. The people try to protect themselves, but their arms and hands are powerless against the flow of liquid, rendered almost invisible beneath the spray and foam. Then, the water pressure drops, and the viewer is now able to see the sodden humans gradually regaining their composure. Other of Viola's artworks, the video titled *The Reflecting Pool* (1977–79), his video installations titled *Tristan's Ascension* (2005, shown at Grand Palais exhibition, Paris, May 2014), and *Acceptance* (2008) are further examples of his creative output that point back to his childhood experience and, to this extent, are thematically coherent with the creative disposition that this earlier experience brought forth and that continues to inform Viola's artistic career. He belongs to a broader pool of artists whose dispositional souvenirs are readily accessible to the public purview.

The second person that I would like to add to this pool is the contemporary British artist Tracey Emin whose oeuvre has, to quote Mandy Merck's research on Emin, so consistently manifest itself in "the literal foregrounding of sex" (119). A notable instance of this broad-reaching trend in Emin's work, is *My Bed* (1998), an installation piece that she first exhibited at the Tate Gallery alongside the other artists who had been nominated for the 1999 Turner Prize. *My Bed* comprises a dishevelled double bed strewn with tampons, used condoms, cigarette butts, empty booze bottles, and other human detritus not typically found in such close concentration outside of rubbish bins and waste transfer centers. Yet, it is here, causing controversy, not in Emin's bedroom but in the gallery space for all to see and to ask each other how this can be called art, and to walk around cul-de-sacs of radical relativism because, of course, one thinks it's art and, therefore, it must be, while respecting differing opinions. A recommendable way out of the stand-off of personal tastes that can hinder critical evaluation, is the more interesting question of how we can expose one or another cultural artifact or action as creative.

Someone walking around Tracey Emin's battle-zone of a bed might well ask what motivates an artist to produce such a work. What drives the artist to such an outcome? What does it tell us about her? This is the kind of insight that Merck offers us in her explanation of the artwork, drawing a direct correlation between it and Tracey Emin's well-documented, traumatic childhood experiences. Emin grew up in Margate, a coastal resort where her mother ran an eighty-room hotel. As Merck explains:

> Abused from the age of eight, raped at thirteen, promiscuous in her early teens, derided as the town slag, she [Emin] has subsequently made this biography (which also includes a suicide

> attempt and the decapitation of a favourite uncle in a car crash) the subject of her work. . . . With *My Bed*, Emin became a prominent figure of personal sexual suffering and public exhibition (often compared to the copyright holder on that situation, Princess Diana) and critics have duly thematized the public and private in response to her work. (120–21)

Beds have an ongoing place along the vast spectrum of subject matter available to artists in the West. A bed-made-art is seen in Vincent Van Gogh's *Bedroom in Arles* (1888)—a beautifully luminous oil painting in which a blood red blanket hangs voluptuously down the side of the bed frame. The photographic series produced by Sophie Calle (whose practice has straddled, and at times toppled off from, the divide between art and stalking) called *The Sleepers* (1979), comprises twenty-three series of 5–12 images showing people that Calle had invited to sleep in her bed, some of whom she knew and others being strangers she had met on the street. Unlike Emin's bed of risk and revulsion, Calle's was one of allure and appeal. The photographic series, *Take Your Top Off* (1993), by Gillian Wearing, who would go on to win the Turner Prize in 1997, and Arthur Smith's play *Live Bed Show* (1995) also belong to this tradition. John Lennon and Yoko Ono's *Bed-Ins for Peace*, a two-week protest against the Vietnam War staged at the Hilton Hotel in Amsterdam in 1969 is another notable example. It would seem that beds communicate a lot about people, just as Georges Perec, the post-WW2 French experimental writer, had a lot to say about beds, specifically his own:

> The bed is thus the individual space *par excellence*, the elementary space of the body (the bed monad), the one which even the man completely crippled of debts has the right to keep; the bailiffs don't have the power to seize *your* bed. . . . I travelled a great deal at the bottom of my bed. For survival, I carried sugar lumps I went and stole from the kitchen and hid under my holster (they scratched . . .). Fear—terror even—was always present, despite the protection of the blankets and pillow. (Perec 16–7)

To those who subscribe to the Neo-Platonist notion of art as that which should lift us out of the banality and entropy of everyday life, offering us an experience of beauty that leads our minds to contemplate a transcendental sphere where we might be united with God, an *art bed* may be that bed that is improved through its translation into art. As philosopher Roger Scruton explains:

> From the beginning of Western civilisation, poets and philosophers have seen the experience of beauty as calling us to the divine. Plato, writing in Athens in the 4th century BC, argued that beauty is the sign of another and higher order. "Beholding beauty with the eye of the mind," he wrote, "you will be able to nourish true virtue and become the friend of God." (qtd. in Lockwood)

There is no God to be found in Emin's bed (unless we count Dionysus, the Greek god of excess and ritual madness), though there is nothing of this celestial absence that has prevented her from calling the bed a beautiful thing. If art made her bed beautiful, like a Greek tragedy can be thought of as beautiful, then I can see why it is enough to make it up in this way and not in any physical manner. Her bed remains unmade and stays artful because of it.

The bed, so far as we can conceive of it as a private space, is encoded via a range of possible meanings: rest; safety; familiarity; comfort; personality; and, given that Emin's bed is a double and not a single bed, hers can also be thought to connote sexuality, intimacy, and companionship. Emin's bed troubles us with a confronting counter-narrative of the bed, connoting not peace but war or, more specifically, with the aftermath of war. It is a bed without idealism, without the romance of the perfect mutually respectful relationship. Emin's bed is a battleground of earthly proportions. The coupling of sex with violence

> is also a familiar theme in many feminist critiques of heterosexuality as well as in psychoanalytic accounts of human sexuality in general. Freud claimed that children perceive intercourse as violence, a "sadistic view of coition" in which the stronger parent is believed to be overwhelming the weaker, and that they experience "obscure urges to do something violent" in early sexual arousal. (Merck 123–24)

Emin rid her home of the bed in a starkly Freudian gesture, bringing what was hidden (and what drew power from this secrecy) out into public view, symbolically as well as literally clearing out a chapter of her life she wished to leave behind, diffusing the aftermath of a relationship breakdown that saw her spend several days in it in a state of self-destructive depression. It is pointless to ask whether a bed should be shown as art, or to be caught up in the status of this art object in a competition. The honesty of the artist's mark, a sign of authenticity so frequently seen in the form of a signature or fingerprint and seen here in the form of an entire domestic setting that is antithetical to the pretentious, staged interiors filling lifestyle magazines, is far more meaningful, far easier to walk around.

It is the honesty of Emin's work, mirrored by the candidness with which she has shared details of her past, that the correlation between her artistic disposition and her childhood experiences seems so direct. In many ways, despite conventional reference to *My Bed* as Emin's bed, maintaining a sense of possession. Although, talking about *My Bed* in 2014, shortly before it was auctioned at Christies, Tracey Emin admitted: "I wish I could keep it, but it's not mine" (Royal Academy of Arts). The bed has not been Emin's bed for a very long time, and this was her intention—to be rid of it—albeit effectively entering it into global mobility, in the beginning at least. This is a mobility made manifest as the life of an internationally touring exhibit (a life it continues to have) and thus, in a sense, denied the opportunity to ever rest again entirely, to fulfill its manufacturer-intended meaning as a context of stasis. Having been dislodged by Emin from its originating place (her bedroom), this unmade-bed-made-art is, shall we say, condemned to a perpetual motion so that it may never again stop long enough to become implicated in (as a stage for) another persons' trauma—condemned to perennial motion. From this esthetic vantage point, it's not clear, nor need it be, whether Emin's bed is being punished or salvaged.

Emin's creative disposition, her foregrounding of sexuality and the dissolution of the boundary between the public and the private, is visible in other examples of her work. Her work *Everyone I Have Ever Slept With 1963–1995* (1995), commonly referred to as *The Tent*, was exhibited in the *Sensation* exhibition held at the Royal Academy in London. This artwork not only invites us to contemplate Emin's sexual past, the emptiness of the tent functioning as a site of empty signification that our imaginations proceed to fill with countless possible scenarios of intimate human entanglement. Sex is power, whoever the barer might happen to be, and Emin uses the politics of sex to challenge other forms of power, such as institutional power. As Julian Stallabrass says: "Tracey Emin wrote an account for 'The Face' magazine about Sensation, teasing the reader with the idea that she might have had 'a good hard fuck' on the steps of the Royal Academy" (212–13). Sex, sexuality, and (the abuse of) power are the subject matter of various other of Emin's oeuvre, such as in *Love Poem* (1996, appliqué blanket): "You put your hand across my mouth. . . . my body is screaming"; such words draw our attention to what Hal Foster calls "the broken boundaries of the violated body" (qtd. in Merck 125). The esthetics of sex are also evident in her diaristic monoprints from the 1990s: *Terribly Wrong* (1997), *Going to Crack* (1997), Scorfega (1997). This was a long time ago, and it is interesting that, while Tracey Emin can be included in an inexhaustible lineage of artists in whom we may detect the childhood seeds of adulthood practices, there is no rule against change (not in life, and certainly not in the context of a mystoriographical investigation). In a recent interview with Alain Elkann, Emin stated of her early work:

> I would never make that work now. It was 21 years ago that I made it and a lot *should* change in 21 years to a person, internally and externally. . . . I can have actually a relationship with someone without sex because I really love them and that love can override all the animal qualities. . . . Yes, my life has really changed a lot, internally it's like a reflection there. Art and life are like a mirror. (Elkann)

I'm sure that there are many creative people who, as adults, pursue practices that are seeded in childhood experience, including the writings of German writer Peter Weiss, whose works are filled with images of the torture and cruelty of World War II from which, it would seem, never ended—images presented to the reader as memories in his narratives, show the presence of the past. As W. G. Sebald explains: "In 1963 Weiss noted that he could say many of his works dated from his childhood, a remark that certainly applies to his subsequent writings and suggests the etiology of the compulsion under which he wrote," such as of an early nightmare of being slaughtered that, through psychoanalytical exhumation, it was later understood, was undoubtedly fueled by "panic terror of an execution" by "the envoys of a superior power to which the child already feels he has been delivered up, and whose agents he recognizes in all figures of authority, but more particularly doctors, who obviously have a professional interest in invading is body" (Sebald, *On the Natural History of Destruction* 176–80). In Weiss's work, as Sebald adds, "acts of mutilation and amputation can be interpreted as pendants to the categorical imperative of memory . . . [b]ecause there is something to be remembered" (Sebald, *On the Natural History of Destruction* 183)..

While this example, and the examples above, might be described as incredible stories, Ulmer recognizes that it doesn't matter if the memory seems insignificant. Who is to tell us what is or is not worth remembering; this is a matter for our own jurisdiction. What do you remember? What haunts you? The detail that sparkles with significance for one person will surely differ to that of another, from moment to moment. As ancient Greek philosopher Aristotle put it, "the aim of art is to represent not the outward appearance of things, but their inward significance" (qtd. in Durant 73). I take this as an appeal to the imagination through which we identify with things, stopping not at how they look (this, instead, is but a starting point), but rather extending our attention to a meditation on what their very presence might mean—their phenomenological aspect.

The aim of the initial *family and memory* stage of the experiment, as Ulmer articulates it, is to remain open to esthetic, gestural, or experiential details from the distant past, letting them bubble to the surface. To the reader, this might seem somewhat at odds with Aristotle whom, to the previous statement, added: "for this, and not the external mannerism and detail, is their reality" (qtd. in Durant 73). For Aristotle, gesture in art is out of the question because it takes place across the surface of objects. However, gestures are often taken as indexical signs, there being a causal relationship between the signifier and the signified (e.g., facial expressions and body language as indexical signs of a person's emotional or psychological state, medical symptoms as signs of disease). In Ulmer's framework, we are always already peering beneath the surface of gestures to gain cognizance of their meaning; we are contemporaneously digging towards art. This said, we are not yet at the point of making value judgments. However, when we go through the process of thinking back to our childhood experiences, it is possible that we will begin to remember things, albeit in slightly altered states, that we had forgotten about; that we as good as lost. Then, once we have remembered these things we are able, in a later stage of the mystory, to make new decisions about what meaning(s) they can hold for us in the contemporary moment, as we move ever more into the future—further and further way from what has been accepted, carried up in the spontaneity of the process, to be the originating points of our attention.

2. Personal (Autobiography)

Neuro-scientific research provides a rational basis upon which to doubt whatever image of the past comes to mind, as if any attempt to note even the most cursory of details can, now, expect to achieve no more authority than the vague under-drawings and indents of a palimpsest that keeps our attention and intrigue while the truth scurries off to lie low elsewhere.

Nevertheless, if I try to conjure up an image from my past that might be used, for better or for worse, as a good enough signifier of an enduring creative disposition, I can remember an unease that distracted me when I was around eleven years old, during my sixth year of primary school, one of several years spent in the bushy Perth hills of Western Australia. Among many happy experiences, it was there that I developed a strange attachment, a psychological fixation that took control of my free time over the course of several months and which, I suspect, has never left me entirely. It was not the sort of attachment that I have heard elsewhere associated with childhood psychological development and fantasy—not as comforting as an object-attachment to a teddy bear or security blanket, or as socially applicable as an imaginary friend that can function as a testing ground for interpersonal relationships. My attachment was seeded in the imagination all the same, and neurotic, but proved to problematize, rather than compliment, how I navigated a physical reality.

When the school bell sounded to mark the start of the lunch break, it would feel as though I had a rope connected to my body at the small of my back and that was somehow, invisibly, anchored in the general space of the classroom. However unusual, in itself this was not so problematic, not even as I ventured out of the classroom door, along the wooden-slatted veranda to the other end where I'd continue down the red-brick ramp, turn left, and enter the sand-bedded playground, for this invisible rope would, in my imagination at least, simply lengthen with each step that I took. By the time that I had been out for ten minutes this hypothetical rope, having started out as little more than an m-dash in my imagination, would perhaps already have grown intangibly to a hundred meters or more, though it is hard to be exact about it thirty years later. However far I went, the rope remained attached to my back, faithfully tracing my perambulations around and inside and back out of the log-built fort, up and down the coarse rope ladders, across the three huge, horizontal truck tires that seemed to have been long since discarded from a mining site far away and yet retained an alluring acrid smell, most noticeable during the full brunt of summer when the sun, having become so hot that the bitumen on the surrounding roads blistered and the pods of the abundant acacia cracked and released their hard, black seeds, would be impossible to rest against when wearing shorts or even to touch with soft, sensitive hands.

No matter what twist or turn I took, no matter how complex a path I drew with my body around the primary school grounds during play time, it was as if the imaginary rope could not fail to take note of it all, documenting everything, archiving, creating a psychological inventory of my meanderings that would invariably haunt me when the time arrived to go back to class, tapping me on the shoulder—prolonged repetitions in the mind. For, when the bell was finally rung, by a student from whichever class that had been assigned bell-ringing responsibilities for that week, a wave of anxiety would reverberate through my body, charged by the knowledge that I would now need to retrace every footstep I had taken or else return to class unraveled, with the playground left in an unmitigated mess.

I would feel the presence of this attachment with increasing acuteness over the course of the forty-five-minute school lunch break, a feeling of urgency that, having begun with the start of the lunchtime bell, would peak as an almost unbearable worry as the lunch break drew to a close, sometimes reverberating into areas of life outside of the pedagogical context.

It is interesting that, long before I had insight to the fallibility of memory, this human nature was something of which I had some tacit awareness. At the end of the play period, when the challenge to retrace my steps was at its peak, I was worried by the possibility that I would not correctly remember where I had been. In this sense, my experience functions as a metonym for that greater play-space of human error. Sometimes, the only way I knew to pre-empt this problem was to restrict my intra-class time movements, during which times I might decide to simply sit on a low brick wall located very near my classroom and which substituted as a solitary waiting station, and listen to the footsteps and voices of the other children as they walked or ran past me, seemingly freely. It was fairly easy to retrace my own footsteps on occasions when I'd only taken ten.

It's strange to think back and notice the extent to which an unrecognized anxiety response was slowly eating away at my physical mobility, a silent enemy of my personal freedom feeding beneath the radar. I suspect that this solitary school-yard practice of tracing invisible lines was an anxiety response to my feeling disconnected from a place of origin, perhaps as an after-image of my migration experience. It would be three decades before I told anybody about it, for no other reason than it became just another piece of the past. As far as my memory holds up today, moving through time in the multifarious spaces of the schoolyard (getting caught up in the games played with others that, in turn, promoted a level of forgetting as to what had been before them) led to a feeling of disintegration—a kind of Platonic entropy. As a young person, completely oblivious of the kinds of theoretical apparatuses that might be used to make sense of it now, I thought that I could strategize around my anxiety by actively limiting how I moved and what I did in a material environment. Thinking back now, it's comparable to the uncomfortable feeling a person might get when they are standing at the end of a long jetty, standing still above deep water, with their eyes closed, in the dark, and then the wind picks up—just the kind of feeling one might be avoiding by sitting on a low brick wall near a classroom in the middle of a still, hot summer's day, as if the mind was now left free to wander.

3. Popular (Community Stories, Oral History, Popular Culture)

The task here is to consider what narrative has made an impression on me, having come from the outside world into the domestic space and intervened in some way. This narrative could be packaged in the form of a movie or a television broadcast or some other kind of media-centric experience that falls under the banner of entertainment, and that articulates cultural mythologies—the wishes, ideas, values, and beliefs of a culture that, through narrative, it reproduces itself.

What do I remember? I remember my family emigrating from England—my country of birth—to Australia in the first half of 1981. By this time, enough early childhood years had passed by for me to have formed, in my mind, lasting images from that life. I was six and a half years old; my two younger siblings were aged two and five and, by their own account, have no recollection of what life was like in Devon—widely regarded as a region of outstanding natural beauty located in the southwest of England—before we moved to the hot and sandy suburb of Padbury located very near the Perth coastline in Western Australia. A year later we left that suburb to live in the semi-arid, bitumen-bubbling hills of Glen Forrest, within the Shire of Mundaring. It's here that I would spend the vast majority of my primary school years, attending the primary school located only meters up the road where, for a period of time, I would spend the last minutes of my recess and lunchtime hurrying around the playground tracing invisible lines.

Among the memories I still have of England, even after more than thirty-five years have passed, there is one in particular that often comes to the forefront of my thinking, appearing unexpectedly like a recurring dream or a limbate soul of a deceased being, a happy haunting. It is a memory with two parts: 1) an instance of entertainment media, and 2) my creative response to it. Of course, I realize that this finds me drawing once more on the family category; it is also a personal memory and one that has been mentioned several times in the context of family conversation. Yet I will persist; today it seems that the two halves are impossible to separate.

The subject and background of my commentary relates to the English singer-songwriter and musician Kate Bush. Kate Bush's debut album *The Kick Inside* was released in 1978, the first single of which was "Wuthering Heights," a song with a meandering melody and lyrics based on Emily Brontë's novel of the same name that was published in 1847—Brontë's only novel. While not her only popular song, "Wuthering Heights" is considered Bush's biggest hit to date; not bad for a song written when she was eighteen years old.

I was almost three years old when the "Wuthering Heights" video clip was aired on British television. The music video released in the UK featured Bush performing in the dark, a blackened void or abyss, with mist filling the space around her feet, which is disturbed and kicked up when she moves her legs, drawing in space while spectral light describes the outline of her head. A second music video, often referred to as the *red dress* version, was produced to accompany the US release of "Wuthering Heights." In this export version, Bush is seen dancing in a green field, with the occasional cloud of fog moving across the frame and a cluster of tall trees in the background.

Most clearly of all, I remember being in the lounge room of the family home (in other countries called a sitting room, living room or parlor). A dominant feature of this room was the rust-red, woolen couch that made my skin feel itchy, and a television located in the corner. But in this memory, I am not sitting in front of it passively ingesting the flittering images and sounds shown in sequence, the syntax and syntagms of mass media communication. In this memory, the "Wuthering Heights" video clip is already playing; I am situated further back in the room, emerging from behind the couch like some kind of Kate Bush wanna-be, holding her up as a tele-visual ego-ideal, in a gesture bordering on the calisthenic with the end of a great long stretch of off-white toilet paper scrunched up tightly in my left hand. I am waving it through the air and around my body as I dance expressively, freely.

This is how I used to watch the "Wuthering Heights" video clip. Yet, this would never be simply an act of watching, as if the eyes were pure, functioning in a state of isolation and amputation from the other senses. As W. J. T. Mitchell says, "there are no visual media."

> "Visual media" is a colloquial expression used to designate things such as television, film, photography and painting, etc. But it is highly inexact and misleading. On closer inspection, all the so-called visual media turn out to involve the other senses (especially touch and hearing). All media are, from the standpoint of sensory modality, "mixed media." (76–77)

Mitchell cites Marshall McLuhan's pioneering work from the 1960s, with McLuhan narrowing the field down to the specificities of television itself. For McLuhan, "[u]nlike film or photograph, television is primarily an extension of the sense of touch rather than of sight, and it is the tactile sense that demands the greatest interplay of all the senses" (in Norden). It is for this reason, as McLuhan puts it, that "TV is not so much an action, as a re-action, medium" (McLuhan 320).

These theoretical insights bare relevance to the physical and psychological experience in which the "Wuthering Heights" video clip took center stage. My improvisational dance was not just about looking and listening but about touch, the texture of the paper, the scratchiness of the woolen couch, the feeling of the carpet on my feet, of the slight breeze produced as I moved the length of toilet paper through the air, the chill of the British winter: these gestural and tactile elements are accompanied by sonic traits, such as the sound of Kate Bush's unusual voice spanning six octaves. Each element adds to the experience of whatever it is that can be seen on the television screen—the void in which she sings.

It is useful to note the way that Bush's waving arms appear as successive, almost instantaneous phases of movements, as do her slow-motion cartwheels—demonstrating a dynamic, video special effect that, as I think of it now, reminds me of the chronophotographic images produced by French scientist Étienne-Jules Marey during the 1880s. Marey invented the *Fusil Photographique*—the world's first portable motion picture camera—because he wanted to record, and study, the locomotion of birds in flight as well as the movements of other animals, including people. Before Marey's innovation, the conventions for representing movement in classical European painting, for example, were strict. The only time that figures were shown to have more than one arm or leg or head was if they literally had more than one. Multiplied bodies, in the classical European tradition, were mythical creatures.

> On the other hand, if a figure is in motion, waving its right arm say, this is never to be conveyed by giving it two right arms (to indicate two stages of the action). This device is sometimes used in a drawing. The idea of breaking down a movement into separate positions wasn't unknown to our ancestors. But between medieval and modern art, the trick is kept out of painting. (Lubbock)

The Italian Futurists took inspiration from early chronophotographic studies by painting movement in their art; an example of this is seen in Giacomo Balla's rather comical *Dynamism of a Dog on a Leash* (1912) and his *Speed of a Motorcycle* (1913), as well as in the repeated red chevrons of Luigi Russolo's *Dynamic Automobile* (1913). Also note-worthy is French artist Marcel Duchamp's painting *Nude Descending a Staircase, No. 2* (1912). Then, nearly seven decades later, I am standing in my family room clutching an absurdly long piece of toilet paper in my hand, watching and mimicking Kate Bush as she waves her arms in exaggerated and provocative miming gestures akin to Lindsay Kemp's *Flowers* (1974). I watch her moving around a misty void space, her absent body made present by the recording medium in ghostly multiplication/duplication. In that imaginative space, she is somehow no longer a mortal woman. Rather, she is a spirit conjured through séance, singing words back to me in a language that I don't fully understand from the impossibly capacious interior of the tele-visual Tardis—like Tiamatu, the primordial ocean goddess of Mesopotamian creation mythology occupying an atemporal and aspatial realm. She is yet to have her skull crushed by the club of the power hungry Marduk, who makes the earth from her bones, the rivers from tears—mother of the cosmic abyss contained within a box within a lounge inside a little house in East Devon.

It is apparent that, although the memory is distant and unavoidably lacking in detail, once we dig beneath the surface of things, there is plenty of material to work with. It is fine that there seems to be precious little to work with here. I will take heed of Hebdige's suggestion, worthy of reiteration, that, in the course of textual analysis (with the *text to be read*, here, being the shifting warp and the weft of memory) attention be directed:

> towards that point—or more precisely, that level—in any given text where the principle of meaning itself seem most in doubt. Such an approach lays less stress on the primacy of structure and system in language ("langue"), and more upon the *position* of the speaking subject in discourse ("parole"). It is concerned with the process of meaning construction rather than the product. (117–18)

I wonder what role the UK version of the "Wuthering Heights" video clip might have played in my emerging creative disposition. It is important to locate information that will further facilitate a critical revisitation of my "Wuthering Heights" memory. We are engaging the imagination, approaching things from a position of parallax. Thus, I shall work around the outside of what I have in mind, encircling it and drawing incrementally closer, I hope, starting by borrowing from widely recognized insight into early childhood development that speaks directly to the development of the imagination. How does it prompt re-evaluation of the sense I make of an image that has remained lodged in my mind since the formative years of my creative disposition? What significance does the length of toilet paper have, given how I used it as a prop with which to dance? What does this object use mean? What insight can it give me about my creative disposition if I approach it in a different way to that path I have so far taken?

The "Wuthering Heights" video clip was first seen on British television only five weeks before my third birthday. This age sits at the boundary of two of the stages of psychosocial development identified in early childhood, as outlined by American developmental psychologist and psychoanalyst Erik Homburger Erikson and which, today, are collectively referred to as Erikson's stages of psychosocial development.

Erikson's (1959) theory of psychosocial development has eight distinct stages. Like Freud, Erikson assumes that a crisis occurs at each stage of development. For Erikson (1963), these crises are of a psychosocial nature because they involve psychological needs of the individual conflicting with the needs of society. According to the theory, successful completion of each stage results in a healthy personality and the acquisition of basic virtues. Basic virtues are characteristic strengths that the ego can use to resolve subsequent crises. Failure to successfully complete a stage can result in a reduced ability to complete further stages and therefore a more unhealthy personality and sense of self. These stages, however, can be resolved successfully at a later time. (McLeod)

Given the dates, it is highly likely that I first encountered Kate Bush, in particular her song "Wuthering Heights," as I was transitioning from stage 2 to stage 3 of Erikson's stages of psychosocial development. Stage 2 relates to the psychosocial crisis of autonomy vs. shame and the basic virtue of will (early childhood, 1½–3 years). During this time, children first start to discover their own abilities and skills, experience an increasing awareness of physical mobility, and "begin to assert their independence, by walking away from their mother, picking which toy to play with, and making choices about what they like to wear, to eat, etc" (McLeod).

English pediatrician and psychoanalyst Donald W. Winnicott also conducted researched in the field of early childhood development, arriving at a theory about the play space of the infant that seems to bare relevance here. Winnicott postulated *potential space* as the place in which the child's imagination starts its development. The child engages in transitional object use, breaking down an illusion of oneness with the mother, thus gaining indelible entry into the symbolic order. For Winnicott, potential space provides the foundation upon which all creativity and cultural experience will be built.

"The infant uses transitional objects to bridge, or affect a passage between the compelling illusion of the unity with the mother and the anxiety produced by the process of separation" (Pigrum 2). He or she "invests specific objects with animate qualities . . . and plays with these objects, talking to them, inventing scenarios for them, filling in the potential space with the child's capacity for imaginative creation and play" (Emigh 2). Furthermore, as Winnicott states, "the use of an object symbolizes the union of two now-separate things, baby and mother at the point in time and space of the initiation of their state of separateness' ("The Location of Cultural Experience" 5). The infant achieves a sense of autonomy through "the filling in of the potential space with creative playing, 'with the use of symbols, and with all that eventually adds up to a cultural life'" (Winnicott Playing and Reality 109).

The age at which I first encountered Kate Bush's "Wuthering Heights" video clip and song sits on the cusp of the third in Erikson's stages of psychosocial development. Stage 3 relates to the psychosocial crisis of *initiative vs. guilt* and the basic virtue of *purpose* (play age, three to five years). Thus, there might be something in the field of child development that helps shed light on the curious image of me dancing around the lounge room with a long strand of toilet paper in my hand, used as a make-shift prop while an audio-visual recording of Kate Bush's singing is being broadcast across the British airwaves. We may come to understand my use of the toilet paper, a kind of transitional object, as a symbolic gesture of triumph over the challenge of bodily functions (like a national flag draped across the shoulders of a marathon winner for one last victory lap), waving it in the air in an improvised dance of freedom, or at least a sense that freedom is within sight, from the external control and influence over one's body—a sense of autonomy framed in art. In other words, the long length of toilet paper is a transitional object that was used to help open out an imaginative space of self-affirming play. I was, effectively, using both the toilet paper and the Kate Bush video clip as a means by which to explore my own sense of autonomy and my emerging capacity to self-govern (i.e., to direct my own goals towards self-actualization.

Engaging in education is one of the most important things that a person can do to become what they desire to be. I feel as if I am approaching a significant synchronicity when I again draw attention to the television located in the corner of the room, but add that, as per my mother's recollections, when I was between two and three years old, she used to sit me down in front of the television to watch the Open University television programmes. She'd let me spend some time sitting there by myself while she used the time to do some housework or to attend to my younger sister.

The Open University television series comprised dozens of "23 minute broadcasts" reflecting a "radical reconstitution of long-established ways of covering subject areas, so as to create short intensive packages . . . [marking out] new terrain . . . between on one hand traditional lectures, seminars and laboratory work and on the other domestic television" (Northedge 1). I will never know for certain which of these programs I sat in front of; I suspect that having the answer to this question would fulfill little more than a trivial concern, though it is possible, at least, to narrow the options down a little. Exposed to Open University content around 1977–78, it is quite likely that I watched an episode from the A101 course, perhaps "An Arts Foundation Course" (1978), broadcast number 18; titled "Visual Music" (Northedge 2). This is the only episode from 1978 included in Andy Northedge's document, and his review is mixed:

> [T]he 1978 A101 broadcast, *Visual music*, presents a very different picture. Instead of a utilitarian studio, we are in Venice, surrounded by magnificent art, architecture and sumptuous music. A well spoken presenter develops a finely crafted treatise on the influence of renaissance music and art upon each other. The interplay of ideas and illustrative examples is impressively polished. However, it is also uncompromisingly sophisticated—assuming easy familiarity with the language and canon of high culture. We are certainly shown the aesthetic and intellectual appeal of the study of classical music but given little sense of being invited to participate. It is a tour de force, but how an entry-level student might engage with the ideas and put them to use is not obvious. It is impressive, but is it teaching? (Northedge 4)

The video-cassette for the Open University's *Visual Music* episode is located in the library of the British Universities Film and Video Council and so, for better or for worse, the meaning-making process in which I am inclined to engage is limited to the information contained in Northedge's review. This said, and as I read its contents, I am genuinely taken aback; does it warrant mentioning that I have a PhD in Visual Arts and, though I still teach in this area, am creatively active as a performing and recording sound artist? Is it significant that my own creative identity is a hybrid of sonic and visual practice? Should I entertain this thought, adding to it the apparent connection between the long past image of Kate Bush dancing in the void and what we might refer to as my own abyss of creative potential? Is it at least partly responsible for the decision, that I would make much later in life, to embark on a doctorate in Visual Arts, concentrating my research on historical and contemporary representations of the abyss—an investigation into abysses of the past, with particular emphasis on creation mythologies? Moreover, is my student-centered approach to teaching practice (informed by Paulo Freire's pedagogical insights and by my own art-educational experience), conceivably, and implicitly responsive to this authoritarianism?

I am uncertain of the so-called truth of these matters; there is still so much more to consider. Nevertheless, Ulmer's mystoriographical process has brought to my attention, in this very moment in time and entirely unexpectedly, a connection I've never previously encountered, and only found now through the very kind of parallax to which I had previously expressed caution, a slip of the hypothetical tongue articulating a return of the repressed, hidden, obscured details pertinent to the uncanny domestic interior (the *heimlich* made, in this moment, positively *unheimlich*). Is the initial seed of my self-identity as an artist, my commitment to facilitating the learning experiences of other artists, inside and outside of institutional architectures, traceable to my watching television in general and to these productions in particular? My relationship with TV is permeated by mixed feelings, and yet I feel more drawn to it now than ever before, driven by an urge to track down this particular episode to see what content in fact it holds, in turn obliterating, beyond any chance of recourse, Ulmer's wish that a lightness of touch be affected in the mystoriographical process (yet I feel that maintaining such an esthetic restraint would betray my own disposition). The glimmer of truth, however fleeting and phantasmagoric, is motivating.

This is the overview as I see it: the lounge room in which I sat as a child, in which I danced with toilet paper, no longer exists. It played an important role in my childhood and, yet, can now only be entered into by way of my imagination. I engaged my imagination, thinking about Kate Bush and her visual music. While in that imaginary space, I looked around attempting to identify any other objects that might have been there. It seems to me to be little more than a futile exercise that might only be redressed if I were to rummage through half-forgotten boxes that contain our family photographs, many of which survive complete with their pinking sheer-cut edges. My recollection features the television in the corner of the room — thus, the most prominent of items, at least prominent enough to trigger another memory. It is this subsequent recollection that led me to the connection between a detail from my past and my creative present, reached through the parallax of memory, approached indirectly. I saw it over the shoulder of a different image, like the past seen through a Sebaldian "glass mountain" (Sebald, *Austerlitz* 224). And, in all of this, the most obvious common denominator is the television set. It may have been a 50cm Monochrome television, model number 6823, popular among middle-class families, sporting desirable features such as "easy slider controls for volume and brightness and instant push-button programme selectors" and a "forward facing speaker" (qtd. in Radios-TV).

In both of these long-term, lingering images of childhood entertainment, the television survives the degradation of cognitive retention as a guiding, mass-media light of the mediated world, and a gateway to the exterior for the scopophilic pleasure of the voyeuristic self, ever stationed at home in the corner of the lounge room, "fully stabilised against mains voltage variations" (qtd. in Radios-TV).

I would have been watching the UK version of Kate Bush's "Wuthering Heights" video clip at around the same time that I was watching Open University programs on the BBC. Both viewing experiences aligned with my transition from stage 2 to stage 3 of Erikson's stages of psychosocial development. Developmentally speaking, therefore, it was during this period of experimentation with autonomy and initiative, advancing awareness of my abilities, skills, and increased physical mobility, using transitional objects to assert independence and, in turn, to locate a sense of personal purpose. I had likely been exposed to art in an educational modality, and one communicated with authority. If this is true, it is also likely that I would have been receptive to authoritative voices, perhaps seeing them as substitute care-givers, captivated by their apparent knowledge and mastery over the unfathomable world. In amongst this is Kate Bush and her creative act, her bodily coordination would have been intriguing to me, given my own developing physical capacities. As a young child, I might not have been able to paint a masterpiece (to be honest, I couldn't even paint one today, and I can't see myself trying), but I could certainly give dancing a go, dancing around freely in my lounge room (as I still often do, now joined by my daughter).

Kate Bush danced almost close enough to touch—as close as she was to hear and to see in the corner of my lounge room, though not quite like the famous Mike TV scene in Willy Wonka & the Chocolate Factory (Stuart). Sensorial, at the very least, she was right there with me, thanks to the magic of television. It's with this in mind that I wonder whether she indirectly, as if through a species of parallax, also functioned as a substitute teacher, the one that speaks not at me but to me through singing and through music, and through her physical mobility. We all recognize the power of a song to teach ideology, that is, to communicate ideas, values, and beliefs (just as a national anthem might be seem to represent the sentiments of an entire nation, sung in classes everywhere; just as we learn our ABCs and other lessons through rhythm and repetition). There is a lesson about art in all of this—a lesson about art in a song about a book, on display for me at a significant time in my childhood development; art is a context of learning and a means to self-determination, not the creation of personal freedom, but rather its articulation.

4. Expert (Disciplines of Knowledge) — Part One

> Interviewer: "Why would anyone want to be an artist?"
>
> David Mabb: "I think it's the nearest thing you come to un-alienated activity." (qtd. in Silver, Ep 1)

There is some flexibility needed when demarcating the third domain of discourse. Fortunately, the mystory thrives on imaginative engagement and improvised invention; flexibility should pose no problem at all.

In his MIT lecture, Ulmer frames this domain in terms of cultural memory and community history within which a person is hailed into a subject-social position. Generally speaking, this could be a local, ethnic, religious, or national community, for example. For this domain, Ulmer has invited mystoriographers to identify the stories/event(s) that the chosen community tells about itself (its mythology) and, as part of this, to identify the protagonist of the remembered event in the cultural history of the chosen community [qtd. in Vardouli, "Gregory L. Ulmer on Mystoriography (Teletheory, 1989)"].

In addition, Ulmer specifies this third domain as an area of expertise, phrased as "disciplines of knowledge" (*Teletheory* 209). This can connote an academic field that, nevertheless, may comprise communities of people who are organized in various ways in relation to that field, directly and indirectly. Whatever our professional field (visual culture studies, literary studies, design-arts, mathematics, chemistry, medicine, etc), a guiding question relating to the third domain of discourse remains: what story does my professional community tell about itself? For me, this is a two-fold picture; it is divalent. On the one hand, it means focussing on a constellation of creative disciplines in which visuality is the most prioritized of all sensory modalities; having participated in tertiary-level design-arts teaching since 2005, I would like to reflect on this realm of professional experience. On the other hand, and given the focus of this creative research monologue, it would be negligent of me to not make mention of my creative output that has existed concurrently, outside of my teaching tasks; nevertheless, the two realms exist in dynamism, in dialogue, despite not always glancing favorably, across critical distance, in the direction of each other. For me, there is no separation of art and the rest of life, and so, while they will be addressed in turn, this is simply a convention of the written exposition. In reality, they oscillate and intertwine, corrupting each other in meaningful ways. It is the purpose of this section to bring this dynamism to light and to make something of it, albeit a radically reduced notion, that can be put towards the formulation of my invariant principle.

> And that blank canvas doesn't have to start blank—I mean, figuratively, not literally. Start small with some sketches. Likewise, a whole novel isn't in your head before you start to write. A plot maybe, a character. Well, write those down and gradually a picture will emerge, the story will begin to unfold. (J. Hegarty 15)

Given my foregrounding of professionalism, I shall begin with a comment relating to the notion of *career*, one that has been playing on my mind as of late, with the expectation that it may help set the tone of the writing to follow. Career/careering: it's interesting that two words so closely spelled can carry such different meanings, as if one is always lurking in the other: *ing*, an Old English suffix denoting "a thing resulting from or produced by an action or process" ("Ing" 1366). From an etymological point of view, at least, making a career out of careering seems like an entirely reasonable prospect.

Conventionally speaking, the career is linear, upwardly mobile and future focused. It is that trajectory of professional activity that a new employee begins at the base of a hill, like Sisyphus on his first day on a job from which he could never be fired, pushing a rock up a hill, or else performing tasks which might be best described via this philosophically-loaded metaphor, such as emptying the bins and doing random tasks. The notion of the career that I grew up with meant something that would take you from a beginning to an end, accumulating meaningfulness in the immeasurable draw towards death. This notion still carries some weight, despite the fact that, today, we live in a post-traditional order, wherein it follows that the invariability of a professional trajectory is like an extinct exotic bird, lost first to the post-modern reality of careering, and then to the mediatory esthetics of meta-modernism.

Careering is about swerving and winding and perambulating crosswise over pathways. It evokes mental images of a person staggering, finding one's feet, staggering again, bumping into others. It means going off track and driving into the ditch, though perhaps not quite like the Italian

Futurist and fascist Filippo Tommaso Marinetti who, having rolled his car during an intoxicated late-night joyride, declared the birth of Italian Futurism and his machine-fuelled fantasies of nationalistic expansion.

Careering means dériving all over the place, heading off a course (having no course), perhaps transitioning from navigating to wayfaring as the beaten path is transgressed and all that is left is the scrub that thrashes the legs that traverse a landscape with a modulated velocity. Careering is nonlinear, unpredictable, akin to a game of snakes and ladders along the course of which we are surprised by events that comprise both advantageous and disadvantageous features, as likely to take us suddenly and unexpectedly forward as they are to trip us up in the sticks . . . stumble trip, stumble trip.

The images that a word like *careering* brings to mind seem to qualify it as an entirely relevant metaphor for practical workings of everyday life. The meritocratic ideal that is central to a democratic, secular social arrangement (after the strictures of Feudal society have eroded), leads us into the problematic belief that people are the sole arbiters of their worldly fate. Meritocracy presumes that, if people work hard enough they will succeed and, inversely, that people are also solely to blame if they fail to achieve their goals (de Botton). It's quite a self-centered ideal or, at least, is one that promotes self-centeredness—by failing to account for the countless others who we will encounter, explicitly and implicitly, seen and unseen, and who will impactupon our lives. People succeed, through hard work as well as luck, just as people fail no matter how hard they might try. We all remain in direct and indirect conversation with forces beyond our control and so, in the dialectic between career and careering, is an oscillation and tension between idealism and pragmatism.

As a teacher of art history and theory, one of the most pervasively detectable themes is the design-arts student's search for confirmation of their own creative authenticity, gained through a kind of perambulation that, specific to the industries in which my students are invested, is sometimes detectable in the work they are trying to produce. It doesn't matter whether we are talking about fashion students, graphic design students, students from visual communications, photo-media or the visual arts, the impulse to know oneself crosses disciplinary boundaries; in each field we find young people expressing the desire to establish a meaningful contribution to their local communities and to the world beyond them. Whatever tools and skill sets they choose to develop, an emotional, physical, and intellectual investment in adding layers of meaning onto this world, through their own actions and of their own volition, is shared.

It might seem vain to search for authenticity, maybe even clichéd, what with authenticity having been a highly cited concern of cultural activity at least since Marcel Duchamp's pan-faced, toilet-humor standoff with New York's Society of Independent Artists in 1917. By purchasing a porcelain urinal at a hardware store and anonymously submitting it for exhibition, Duchamp delivered his institutional critique deadpan. A Society board member, Duchamp was cognizant of the material and ideological contexts in which he operated; his urinal made comment on the modern West's preoccupation with an ideal of the unique artist, their singular works, and the systems that employed them, commissioned them. He knew this circumstance was arbitrary; as David Inglis says, the notion of the uniqueness of an artist "endowed with a special 'artistic' vision of their own, dates primarily from the early nineteenth century . . . Indeed, the ideas of 'art,' 'artworks' and 'artists' are not just modern inventions but are specifically Western inventions too" (91). To take Mikhail Bakhtin's notion of the *utterance* as non-autonomous in its direct or indirect responsiveness to other utterances, the meaning of Duchamp's urinal remains contingent on its historical location; history spoke through it (71). In this sense, we detect an appeal to authenticity that emerges not simply from Duchamp's direct antagonism with institutionalized art but from the dynamism between a cultural statement, its histories and its possible futures.

Duchamp's appeal to authenticity reflected his capacity for cultural reflexivity and was something quite apart from the need to demonstrate technical mastery. If Duchamp could accuse the modern West of privileging pre-existing ideas around artistic production, the grounds upon which such privilege stood were rather thin for it was only ever protecting a historical anomaly. By presenting, via his artwork, an unambiguous challenge to the fiction of artistic privilege in the modern West (to the idea that good art represents the best of the best that culture has to offer), Duchamp was not so much undermining authentic principles of creative production, but rather returning to them. For Duchamp, exposing the arbitrariness of an elitist notion of art, "wanting to get rid of the word art altogether," was the honest thing to do (Zola). To place a urinal in a gallery was, oddly, to activate an ethical and moral gesture. As Duchamp explained:

> Mr Mutt's fountain is not immoral, that is absurd, no more than a bathtub is immoral. It is a fixture that you see every day in plumbers' shop windows. Whether Mr Mutt with his own hands made the fountain has no importance. He CHOSE it. He took an ordinary article of life, placed it so that its useful significance disappeared under the new title and point of view—created a new thought for that object. (qtd. in Taylor)

The urinal was not made by Duchamp; it was a completed object when he found it, only to then be displaced by him in a way that its capacity to function not as a urine receptacle but as an art object was exposed, akin to the tale of the Emperor's new clothes wherein the status-centric delusion is denuded. The urinal never showcased Duchamp's technical skills, but rather his integrity as a cultural communicator; for Duchamp, creativity was not simply about making stuff but about recognizing opportunities to communicate in an innovative and critical manner. A century later, this particular creative utterance, the urinal, a constant reminder of Duchamp's capacity to demonstrate personal choice, against the grain, is widely regarded as the modern world's greatest work of visual art (Gleitman, Fridlund, and Reisberg).

The place of authenticity in the arts-related institution is a matter of ongoing relevance. Artistic activity is still institutionalized and it is still available for critique, not least of all when there is ambiguity along the spectrum of, on the one hand, seemingly autonomous creative endeavor and, at the other end, thoroughly industrialized, commercially driven productivity, with a vast spectrum stretching between the poles. Wherever it is that we locate different practices on this spectrum, our own practices or the practices of others, our evaluations will be informed by our understanding of the social value of art, in view of our professional proximity to the conditions of capitalism within which we perform our creative, cultural acts.

Artistic authenticity survives as a pre-eminent value in contemporary arts-related practice that provides a "framework for self-actualisation" (Giddens *Modernity and Self-Identity* 9). Revisiting the work of German neurologist and psychiatrist Kurt Goldstein, Abraham Maslow (383) defines *self-actualization* as "the desire for self-fulfillment, namely the tendency for him [the individual] to become actualized in what he is potentially. This tendency might be phrased as the desire to become more and more what one is, to become everything that one is capable of becoming."

Thus, creative modes of productivity locate authenticity in humanistic actions and run parallel to "the full realization of one's potential (qtd. in Gleitman, Fridlund, and Reisberg). Niaz Murtaza's findings that "self-actualization leads to the highest form of human welfare" places self-actualizing practices high up on the list of basic human needs (579). Much more than a *want*, I would go so far as to say that authenticity, as an honesty to the self and of the self, is a basic human right, under any ideological, material, or economic circumstances.

The notion of living truthfully to oneself is an undeniably serious matter, taken as such in mystoriographical work. Let us spend time with this, therefore, taking a moment with Kurt Goldstein's view that self-actualization is "the tendency to actualize, as much as possible, individual capacities, its 'nature' in the world" (Maslow 196). As an artist, I recognize Duchamp's still-relevant lesson that authenticity is advanced through creative work that shares critical insight into a relationship between personal choice and the conditions under which such choices are made; that it necessitates a degree of courage and resilience. Here, I use Robert E. Franken's definition of creativity as "the tendency to generate or recognize ideas, alternatives, or possibilities that may be useful in solving problems, communicating with others, and entertaining ourselves and others" (396). These models of thinking are brought together in Robert Nelson's view that the practices by which new ways of living are legitimately investigated and made available for contemporary public debate lend themselves to creative authenticity:

> If true to consciousness—or some earnest reflection of experience—art is bound to be original. We know the measure of our capabilities: we negotiate afresh the mix of form and content. It will infallibly result in distinctiveness, at least originality at the margin, though this may not in itself grip the world. Bringing consciousness to life in your own language is reliably authentic and original to qualify as new knowledge; but its significance lies on the ontological side, where it prompts the further life and growth of someone else's intelligence of the world and themselves. (Nelson 99)

Of course, much work has been done since Duchamp, work not limited to the creative and intellectual pursuits of white Western European males. Nevertheless, Duchamp's urinal has provided creative practitioners throughout the world with a prototypical model of critical self-awareness and a call to arms for authenticity in the visual arts—a call suited to the dynamic, conditional, and post-traditional order that modernity continues to be. Perhaps a conversation built on the legacy of Duchamp would seem digressive if this model did not have implications for all fields of creative endeavor, from the esoteric to the mainstream—the conceptual to the technical, the avant-garde and experimental to the commercial and the predictable.

Having received arts training that, ironically, is in keeping with the legacy of Duchamp's institutional critique, for me, creativity is an opportunity for vital agitation, for the purpose of exposing what bubbles beneath the crust of habituation and certitude, starting with personal experience and thinking about how this relates to a more broadly shared cultural condition. Art, for want of a better word, is an opportunity to engage in a cultural conversation that promotes critical reflection on the circumstances under which we live our lives and, most specifically, under which we imaginatively express ourselves. It is with this background, a bias towards a kind of sociological art, that I enter the classroom as a teacher of art history and theory to tertiary-level design-arts students. These are students who, whatever their personal ambitions, are sitting in a classroom that belongs to a proudly industry-driven institution that seeks to advance its industry currency. All of the apparatuses are put in place that confirm, for the institution's young adult customers, that they have made the right choice in committing time and money in training that will help them, one day, fulfill the labor demands of the creative industries. Industry-relevance is crucial for the viability of an institution geared towards producing graduates who have demonstrable capacity to go out into the outside world and be successful as part of a highly competitive workforce and attract clients. In short, the raison d'être of a design-arts institution is to produce graduates in possession of the specific attributes that see them prepared for industrialized labor or, in Marx's widely referenced terms, for alienation. As Phil Gasper explains:

> A reason why alienation occurs under capitalism is that capitalism is an economic system in which a small minority controls the means of production, and in which most people can survive only by selling their own labour power. Workers under capitalism have to work for someone else. As a consequence, Marx argues that work has little or no intrinsic worth for the worker—as he puts it, "it is not the satisfaction of a need but a mere means to satisfy needs outside itself." ("Capitalism and Alienation")

Marx's focus is on the workforce as a taker of lives that it does not fully observe, which in this instance is the labor-space post-graduation. Attending to the contemporary moment, we can ask: how might we critically consider the design-arts classroom to pave the way for this kind of outcome? Why don't the students revolt? Maybe some semblance of an answer exists in a broad notion of the classroom that comes from French Sociologist Pierre Bourdieu. Bourdieu's thoughts on the classroom pique my interest because of his attempt to reflect upon student agency. Speaking of the way that girls seemed to do better in schools than boys, Pierre attends to the myth that females outperform their male peers because they develop earlier, so that their achieving higher academically is commonly credited to a naturally advanced maturity and intelligence (Carles). However, Bourdieu challenged this idea, arguing that females tend to do better than males in educational contexts because they are, from an early age, trained to be more docile—to do what the teacher wants them to do (Carles). Making females docile, to cite the dictionary meaning, entails making them submissive to training or direction, not assertive; easily managed" (717). Bourdieu reminds us that the word *docile* comes from the Latin word *docilis*, which means *ready to follow instruction*. Bourdieu explains that females are not naturally better, but rather are taught to behave in a way that is in keeping with the values of a patriarchal society. He observes that the submission of female students is counter-balanced by a greater tolerance for male misbehavior, encapsulated in the phrase *boys will be boys* (Carles).

Bourdieu is admirable in his criticism of the patriarchal classroom and supporters of Feminism everywhere may applaud his attempt to expose patriarchal oppression. This said, I cannot help but spot the implication that young women not be credited for their own achievements, even partially. Bourdieu's point may alternatively be read as a kind of back-handed compliment, whereby it is with thanks to the patriarchy that young women do as well as they do, as early as they do, and that without the directive underhand of patriarchal oppression, we are left with a question around what the basis of a young woman's achievement might be.

I appreciate that we are entering into a rather wobbly notion, and it forces me to intensify mindfulness of my own teaching style because the very last thing that I would ever want to do is to dominate the very same students whose creative capacities I wish only to support. Then again, there are curricula—governed, mandated, enforced, linked into policy, and policy is expressive of the demands of the powerful groups whose role it is to ensure that institutions meet the economic needs of a nation. In a broader context of education and training, we can appreciate Bourdieu's overarching message regarding skill—that our notions of skill, and the various self-evaluations that follow on from these ideas, are embedded in contexts of power; that the evaluation of skill is a function of ideology. To put it another way, we understand ourselves through things over which we have only partial control, even if we maintain a high level of choice in the sense-making process. Thus, our notions of creative ability are directly and indirectly impacted upon by the ideological contexts in which we communicate them, either verbally or through the products of our physical labor. Regardless of whether we are teachers or students, dominant ideologies peep into, and inform, our professional spaces. They help to shape any opportunities for creative cultural negotiation that we may encounter within (personal studios, school work areas, work-placement pathways, competitive arts-related activities, etc).

Bourdieu's insight is now several decades old. Today, in a world where we are empowered through the learning that comes from conversations with the constellation of gender identities represented by LGBTIQAN+ communities, it is not enough to speak simply of boys and girls and is to not appropriate to entertain any gender privileging inside or outside of the classroom. Everyone has the right to quality education. I am fortunate enough to be employed by an institution that shares this fundamental respect and welcomes an evolving understanding of our students. We recognize that it is not always clear how we can appeal to the value of equality while, at the same time, and in practice, sufficiently accommodate the diverse educational needs of our diverse student cohort. However, someone taking a Marxist perspective could say that what we have is an openness to prepare all walks of life for industrialized alienation. A Bourdieuean conclusion to draw, from this perspective, might be that all students are now equally encouraged to be amenable to instruction; with the playing field more than ever directed towards the goal of equality, Bourdieu might express concern that all students are included in training towards *docilis*.

It should be said that, in my experience of design-arts teaching in the Australian context, an ever-present respect for gender diversity in the classroom and an emphasis on the empowerment of students is critical. It is interesting to note that women practitioners comprise by far the largest group throughout the visual arts sector—from hobbyists to professionals. This is a current insight, but not a new one; an Australian study conducted by David Throsby and Anita Zednik has shown that approximately two thirds of professional visual artists (sixty-three percent) and four-fifths of craft practitioners (seventy-nine percent) were women (Throsby and Zednick 22). Thinking back to my classrooms, I'd say the figures are even more extreme; throughout the past decade, on average, at least ninety percent of my students have been females between eighteen and twenty-five years old (coincidentally, this the approximate age range during which Kate Bush went from being an unknown song writer to being an international celebrity). This demographic percentage is an average that accounts for an estimated total of 1400 students that I have taught across this time period. On occasion, I have had classes with no males in them; the ninety percent observation is current and relative to the entire student population with which I come into pedagogical contact. In view of these numbers, when I recall Bourdieu's accounting for the achievements of female students, I am reminded of my own responsibility; it informs the attitude with which I seek to support the positive educational experiences of my students.

My pedagogical role has largely been to introduce students to various critical concepts that have impacted significantly on the creative arts. A key part of this education is helping students make practical sense of some of these (feminisms, fetishisms, ideologies and propaganda, post-colonialisms) in the context of their own personal and emerging professional lives. It is a secular education that encourages critical self-evaluation that some might refer to as risky-thinking. So, however we might frame the truth of the matter to which Bourdieu draws our attention, I cannot help but worry, avoiding hypocrisy in my willing to walk the talk and reflect upon my workplace and, albeit sometimes in an unnecessarily ruminative manner, invent stories about the impact of industry-driven education on the activities, energies, and potentialities of young women, for whom education is an opportunity to establish a professional identity within the broader community and, quite likely, assess their socialized sense of self-worth.

During an in-class conversation on Bourdieu's notion of cultural capital, the female students reported experiencing difficulty articulating the value that they bring to society. It is one thing for me to respond by reassuring them that, from a pedagogical perspective, it is clear that they are energetic, and far more open to new ideas than I ever was at that younger age, that they are articulate and caring and concerned about the vast unknowns of the futures awaiting them in their technologically sophisticated, industrialized society. I can say this stuff, and maybe they will show understanding of the meaning of my message, but that is only a small part of the sense-making equation; it remains that they have trouble seeing this for themselves. "We haven't had much life yet," was the consensus. This is true, and lucky for them, but being young doesn't mean that you have less value or less to contribute, does it? For me, it means you have more potential; more ahead of them to look forward to realizing. Without a clear sense of their own ontological and epistemological anchorages, perhaps they remain impressionable under the bright lights and ambitions of authorities in positions of cultural power.

In some ways, this point about *docilis* is true of a lot of education; displaying a degree of docility in class, not behaving in a manner that impacts negatively on the safety and activities of others, not disrespecting others' rights, is a common-sense part of conducting oneself appropriately in any shared-learning environment. In this sense, what Bourdieu calls *doing what the teacher asks* is about being a conscientious student of any subject matter—about taking seriously one's skills and responsibilities as communicated by the authorities of one's discipline. Training is in part about acculturating oneself to industry standards. Yet, according to Richard Taylor (119), creativity is "done not by rule, rote, or imitation, but with successful originality," and offers a path to true fulfillment. There is a tension here, around the outcomes expected of differing models of creativity. Taylor seems to be implying that fulfillment comes from rule-breaking, or at least from a purposeful disregard for rules. It raises the question of what scope an emerging creative professional has to rule-break when they are being paid to meet the briefs of a corporation? If there is any fulfillment to receive, who receives it?

Let's think back to Marx, about the labor context under capitalism. For Marx, workers remain vulnerable, though they may be unwittingly complicit in it, to exploitation. Capitalism means exploitation because it is about making the most of the resources at hand in order to extract the maximum possible profit out of them, and a rhetoric of resource exploitation does not exclude human resources. Is this not what we all admit to doing when we say that we work hard to make the most of our lives? On a personal level, I'm doing it now, digging up of myself what I can to move forward in a meaningful way; committed to my own creative industriousness, I am willfully exploiting myself, putting to work memories of which I can never claim to hold full possession, and I'm thoroughly enjoying it.

Historically speaking, industrial exploitation has been given a dismal appraisal. In *Kapital*, Marx's definitive critique of capitalism, he alerts us to a children's commission report from 1863. As economics journalist Paul Mason says:

> and there's a nine year old kid working a fifteen hour day. Marx looks at that and he understands that in that story lies the whole secret of how the system works. The secret of capitalism is this idea of surplus value. Where does profit come from? Marx says it comes from work. When this little boy turns up to work, everything that's gone into getting him there — the food, the clothing, maybe the education, certainly the housing — costs some money, and his labour is worth all of that. But the amount of work he does during that working day, that fifteen hour working day, is way above what he needs to. And the difference between what it should take, what his work is really worth, and what he's actually working is a surplus. That's where profit comes from and we know, actually, that he is trawling through this stuff for these acute examples of exploitation, because he wants to shove the concept of exploitation right down the throats of mainstream economics. Mainstream economics, then and today, doesn't even accept that exploitation exists. When a factory falls on the head of a bunch of Bangladeshi garment workers, that's an accident; to Marx, it's one of the most fundamental laws of capitalism, that the capitalist will extract the maximum amount of surplus value that they can. (qtd. in Cowling)

Marx is concerned with the conditions of the working class under capitalism and, while the given example is of a child, it is a model of thinking applicable to laborers of all ages and of the challenge that capitalist society poses to creative freedom. For Richard Taylor, there a lot at stake:

> All this points to a kind of imperative, minimally expressed as: Do something. Better expressed, it says: Create something. To do otherwise is simply to waste your precious life. Do not rest upon your dead kinship with the beasts. All they do is eat, sleep, reproduce, then die and decay. For a person to do no better than that is in effect to lapse into a mere animal nature. (qtd. in Academy of Ideas)

On a marginally more optimistic note, I should hasten to add that, having once upon a time gone through an undergraduate art degree of a somewhat similar (albeit a distinctly non-commercial) form, I appreciate that whatever happens at art school will not inevitably dictate a person's subsequent art-related activities. Art education is not a life sentence; only a small percentage of graduates go on to enjoy full-time creative career(ings), and there are many non-art-related fields to which creative thinking skills can be applied (I met my wife when we were both at art school, me annexed away in the painting and her a textiles major. She is now Deputy CEO of a primary healthcare network, and still enjoys applying her creative problem-solving skills on a daily basis).

Thinking back to those times, even though I remember being interested in the theory classes and in the feedback sessions during which my peers and I tried to reflect critically on each other's projects, I have absolutely no recollection of what those conversations entailed. I vaguely remember numerous social gatherings, a few pieces of work that I made and that I felt proud of. I also recall feeling completely overwhelmed by the demands of theory classes that I suspect, twenty-five years later, were probably not that challenging to begin with. What I remember clearly is the impulse (fostered by our lecturers) to produce honest work—instilling in us an understanding that authentic creativity was important.

Maintaining authenticity requires an ongoing critical self-transparency. It is standard promotional practice for educational institutions of all kinds to position themselves in the market place (which may or may not be graced with the presence of Nietzsche's Socratic-esque figure of the madman) as if what they had was precisely what prospective students needed in order to get where they want to go, even if those students don't quite know where that is. They read the brochures, are impressed by colorful, high-gloss images contained therein.

Of course, art schools don't hold a monopoly on creativity, and it would surely be sad if they did. There are too many artists to count, including the modernists who either ran kicking and screaming from the art schools, or else declared very early on their autonomous affiliations. Perhaps we should suppose they are cynics, blinded by their own biases (as if bias was undesirable), and thus think for a moment about what institutions of art have to say about themselves; let's attend to their self-promotions. What claims do they make of themselves? What message do they use to fish for an attentive audience—their potential students?

The school motto remains one of the most important motifs of institutional visibility; it is designed to reflect a school's identity—their public face encapsulated in a single phrase that, thus, attests to its competitiveness. What's in a name? "Dream Large" is the message underscoring Melbourne University's Model degrees; Edith Cowan University's is "Reach Your Potential"; La Trobe University has "Qui cherche trouve" (French) [Whoever seeks shall find]; Deakin University's home page displays, in the imperative mood also employed in the other examples mentioned, "Start here today. Go anywhere tomorrow"; the Academy of Design, Australia says "Make it happen!" In the case of the latter, this motto replaced "Anything is possible inside the Academy" after the Academy joined the LaSalle College International Education Network in 2015. It was definitely an improvement on the old official claim; I always felt a little unsettled by its quasi-religiosity, as if the place in which we worked was not a converted warehouse in a semi-industrial area, next door to an Oleo product manufacturer that frequently filled the breeze with strong wafts of raw meat, but rather a transcendental zone — much like a cathedral or some other place of worship where, just by crossing the Westwork, the fee-paying entrant is magically whisked away from the realm of normal behavior and imminence (like Dorothy getting whisked off my hot air to Oz) and into a Tardis-like spatial paradox. The motto "Anything is possible inside the Academy," seemed to make the paradoxical claim that creative potential is boundless, albeit within the finite boundaries of the institution.

The fact that this motto didn't make any sense didn't actually matter because, even in paradox, its sentiment was no less crystal clear. It was, like all good propaganda slogans, empty; it's precisely this emptiness that allowed the viewer, any viewer, to read into it whatever they wished and, therefore, permitted a potential customer's meaningful connection with the institution on the level of a personal ideology, on the level of extant socialized, and now reinforced, hopes for and dreams of a better future. Institutional mottos are idealistic; they reproduce and normalize the meritocratic ideal, thus justifying skills-based self-centeredness (which is my short-hand for self-worth that is measured in accordance with the social value of one's acquired abilities, their industry-specific recognition/institutional validation, etc). Sometimes these institutional slogans are grandiose in their implicit declarations of self-importance, and on the surface of it seem preoccupied with fantasies of unlimited success, power, or brilliance—a practice neither uncommon nor economically indefensible, in some way reliant on the viewer feeling dissatisfied with the present state of their life. This doesn't mean, however, that it's honest and, so far as a slogan finds its institution appealing to what it desires, ultimate power and success gained through competitive marketing strategies, it doesn't strike me as particularly robust foundation for authenticity. "Design Your World" is the motto under which we now operate; the verb *design* is presented in the imperative form, creating a sense of urgency for personal power and control over one's chosen domain.

Kate Bush never went to art school. I did, and in many ways I never really left. Though, the school in which I am a teacher seems radically different from the one in which I was a student, and there is little wonder as to why; I once saw things purely from a students' perspective and, somewhere in the middle of two decades, I found myself standing on the other side of the mountain. When I went to art school, I was one of 137 full-time fine arts students in a learning environment that was decidedly non-commercial, even anti-commercial. The focus there was on artistic rigueur and, in some ways, it was as if students were expected to metaphorically bleed for their art. Students were not encouraged to pursue any commercial activity and, in fact, those who worked in the artisan vein were noticeably shunned. Skills were learned independently on a need-to-know basis. Students pursued personal practices and sourced the skills required for that practice to evolve.

In contrast, an art school like the Claremont School of Art (Western Australia)—where my wife, Julie, had previously studied—was thoroughly dedicated to pushing an artisan approach to art making; every class was useful, she told me, whether it be focussed on bronze cast making, or how to mix egg-based painting mediums. By the time I returned to my own art school a decade later as a PhD candidate and began my foray into teaching, although the pedagogical philosophy had not changed a great deal, which was at least partly to do with the fact that many of the same teachers were still working there, the full-time fine arts student numbers had dwindled to less than fifty.

My understanding of creative education has changed as my function within it has changed. Could this ever have been in question? After all, I went from being a student in a non-commercial environment (and spent my early teaching years there also), to being a teacher in an overtly commercial environment—where the fine arts students are a minority, perhaps even an anomaly. Yet, several characteristics that I would have readily accredited to those *good old days*, can still be witnessed today:

dedicated teachers wanting the very best learning experiences for their students often become tired teachers visibly worn down by semester's end from their emotional and intellectual investment in the duties associated with providing quality education and dedicated students who want to make the most of their time often become tired and stressed students, some of which will approach you on assessment days in tears, visibly worn down by the responsibilities associated with receiving quality education.

What hasn't changed are the students who struggle and the students who cruise through. What hasn't changed is the incredible luxury of having interested peers providing critical feedback on tap. What hasn't changed are the worries and wonders and problems that young people have writing essays. I was one such student who found writing essays a nightmare; I remember once, as a second-year degree student, having to provide a piece of writing on my own creative project, which I ended up submitting in two parts—(1) a free-form poem about sneaking under the Fremantle harbor jetty at night, balancing on the pylons just above the then black heaving water and about watching the industrial-sector lights flickering and dancing on the horizon and (2) not confident that this esthetic artifact would be enough, a rather vague but thankfully short expository ramble that tried to explain it all away in an argumentative language in which I had no confidence. I received a mark of fifty-one percent and the unambiguous advice that if I have submitted just the poem and nothing more I would have gotten a better mark. I am not self-centered enough to imagine that my experience is unique and so take my struggle, beyond the finer details, as shared. What also remains shared is a desire to reach one's goals, even if they don't quite really know what they are.

As an art history and theory teacher, a significant part of this role entails introducing students to important ideas about culture and asking them to develop critical responses in the form of research essays. Often, the first stop is to explain to students what the word *essay* actually means, for many of them by then have written essays and developed a distaste for writing, yet without thinking about what they are actually supposed to be doing (the word *essay* comes from the French verb *essayer*, which means *to try, to attempt*). I try to reassure students by sharing my challenged past (quite often also the present) and use this as a basis of empathy that informs how I listen to their concerns and how I help them overcome their hurdles.

Industrialized creativity is competitive. Across my experience of working in tertiary level creative education, I have noticed a profound institutional interest in capturing the *good stories* of students, particularly those who have graduated and that who, I suppose by way of their own extra-curricular efforts, may be deemed fit to be drawn back into the corporate fold in worldly validation of the apparatus still in operation. This is fine if what is important is every next opportunity to self-applaud, a kind of parasitic marketing. The good story works well on a promotional poster and, like the countless disappointing *selfies* from among which only the most flattering photo is selected for online dissemination, so too does a focus on the good story play into the game of false representations. Reward for successes is fine but, in any competitive field, the winner stands alone on the podium, distanced from the others by their institutionally validated achievements.

Why, as the old idiom goes, are winners also grinners? Is it a smugness that comes from believing in one's own membership to a minority population, lifted up from the great mass by virtue of their success? This makes the majority a suitable target audience for the good stories that exclude them and remind them of their shortcomings. As Alain de Botton puts it, "[t]he modern world is based around the idea that we're all essentially equal . . . we most envy people who tend to be our equals. In a world in which everyone is supposed to be equal, but where there's still a lot of inequality around, it's hard not to take the achievements of others as an implicit reproach for everything you don't have and haven't done" (Status Anxiety). Stories told by winners on podiums are stories told into a microphone as part of an award acceptance speech (a special kind of megaphone for a special kind of story), there constituent ideas, values, and beliefs transmitted through loud speakers and into the auditory canals of those who "cannot listen away as one can look away" (Connor 133). What sense might we make of this? At least in R. Murray Schafer's terms, the scene is problematic:

> Imperialism is the word used to refer to the extension of an empire or ideology to parts of the world remote from the source. It is Europe and North America which have, in recent centuries, masterminded various schemes designed to dominate other peoples and value systems, and subjugation by Noise has played no small part in these schemes. . . . When sound power is sufficient to create a large acoustic profile, we may speak of it, too, as imperialistic. For instances, a man with a loudspeaker is more

> imperialistic than one without because he can dominate more acoustic space. A man with a shovel is not imperialistic, but a man with a jackhammer is because he has the power to interrupt and dominate other acoustic activities in the area. (In this sense we note that outside workers were able to improve their position remarkably after they were in possession of tools to attract attention to themselves. No one listens to a ditch digger.) (77)

However we might criticize the implicit imperialism of competitive contexts and, to this extent, the drive towards elitism that they promote, it is important to recognize other peoples' achievements. We can engage in respectful recognition without resorting to methods that are inter-personally divisive, and while including in this recognition of the far bigger picture of human experience for which a trophy or oversized cardboard check do not adequately account. Thus, although I may be swimming upstream, I am not as enthusiastic about hearing the good stories as I am about hearing the bad ones. I want to hear about the person who made a mistake or failed but who, through their creative capacities, managed to find a way forward (the most interesting experimental music gigs I have attended have been those where something has gone wring half-way through—during which an aspect of a performer's gear has broken down or where they have lost all sound completely. In such instances, the audience ends up watching not the practiced, manicured reiteration of what might have been rehearsed at home, but rather the performer's necessary creative and immediate problem-solving abilities (i.e., who they really are as an artist).

Given my participation in the experimental music scene here in Melbourne, it might not surprise you that I should now share a sound-art-related anecdote, augmenting the scope of my professional domain of discourse. I will use this augmentation as an opportunity to reflect on the issue that is at hand around *skill*, thus enabling a narrative arc—from a point of critical distance—back into the tertiary design-arts classroom where thinking around creative authenticity is re-engaged.

It is common for listeners to assume that experimental music does not involve preparation. This is a possibility rather than a rule. Most obviously, the prepared piano works of John Cage are but a mere glimpse into the vastness that is the careful selection and treatment of resonant and non-resonant objects for their subsequent application in a sonic presentation. Just thinking of the contributions made by my peers in this community, including Lara Goodall's cassette tape manipulations, Todd

Anderson-Kunert's tonal explorations, Sean Baxter's junk percussion, the forays into percussion processing made by Nat Grant, Ari Sharp's television feedback sculptings, Anthony Cooley's walls of drone, among the diverse audible forms produced by many others, locally and internationally: none of these are thoughtless acts. Each performance is the expression of a broader investigative practice that, throughout the course of time, leads to the artist developing a highly personalized, idiosyncratic repertoire of skills that are immediately applicable in a live music scenario that can be described, as Sean Baxter has phrased it, as a way to "fight against boredom in music."

Much like the relationship between a designer's creative output and the effort invested in its production, a live performance will likely expose merely the tip of the ice-berg of a person's entire practice, assuming the artist chooses to perform or exhibit their work at all. A few weeks ago, I watched a short video in which Sophie Giles, an architecture lecturer at the University of Western Australia, explained that

> the typical architect who doesn't teach would be involved in probably a number of scales of project. So, small scale projects, possibly drawing designing details, working on-site fielding calls from contractors on site, working in large teams, large projects either locally or around the world. I think sometimes architects wish they could just sit down in one spot and design all day. Architects are generally covering a whole lot of different scales of project at the same time. Sitting down to draw would be a luxury. (Student Edge)

Although made in reference to a different area of expertise, Giles's comments are applicable to many fields of endeavor in which limited room for creativity is typically framed by various forms of effort. Relating this back to sound-art, these efforts might contribute to the fight against boredom in music while remaining, themselves, largely unseen.

It is incredibly interesting, for me, therefore, to be at a live experimental music event as a member of the audience and, perhaps five minutes into a 20–25 minutes set, witness a veritable breakdown in the performer's equipment. For example, on the evening of December 11, 2013, I was at the Barley Corn Hotel in Collingwood, there to perform as part of an experimental group called the *Royal Melbourne Noise Choir*. Other acts on the bill included Nik Kennedy whose *Smasmoslop* project sees him feeding vocals through quite an impressive array of effects units, such as delays and bit crushers and filter boxes. He has a board that's about 120 centimeters by 50 centimeters completely packed with these devices and with the mass of patch cables required to connect them in esoteric ways, all held up in front of him by a keyboard stand. The first time I saw Nik perform, he came out in a black cloak and aviator goggles, microphone headset in place to ensure both hands remained free to twist and turn the dials before him like a mad professor performing sonic alchemy. The first noise he made, on this memorable occasion, was a roar of such ferocity (no doubt shaped and augmented by the gadgets through which the sound waves had to pass before being projected at high volume from the venue's speaker system and into the variously protected ear canals of the audience) that one could easily forget what a gentle human he really is.

In any case, at the Barley Corn Hotel, we were only a few minutes into a *Smasmoslop* performance of almost equal intensity and, all of a sudden, the whole place fell into near silence—only the sounds of clinking glasses behind the bar and a few gasps from the punters in front of it could be heard. Nik had lost his signal, and no one seemed to know why, including him. So, for the next five minutes, which understandably seemed like far longer, we remained watching as quiet-as-a-mouse Nik's eyes darted around his set-up, checking and double-checking the audio pathways he had previously connected, his hands disconnecting cables, reconnecting cables, moving things around, checking power supplies, looking around the table-top, looking beneath it, trying a few dials, a latching switch, a momentary switch, more cables unplugged, more cables reattached. As we watched throughout those elongated minutes, as Nik was perhaps suffering extreme anxiety and indeterminacy, all I could think of was how wonderful it all was. I do not mean this in a *schadenfreudian* way, but rather I was genuinely engrossed in the glorious image of an artist now working incredibly hard on-the-spot, and under considerable creative pressure, to confront his *not-knowing* and to overcome it, thus emerging on the other side, resuming his delivery of formidable inundations of sound. For me, this was truly improvisational, the side of the creative process (much like the mixing of paint that takes place as the painter prepares to do work) that is often left out of the picture, the activity we intellectually understand must take place, because we might see evidence of it in the final outcome, but which is typically not put on show. But, because so much of an experimental sound-based practice can take place outside of the performance space, I found this short period of error and disintegration, this problem demanding immediate and creative negotiation, greatly interesting. I was seeing what was usually hidden. I was seeing something private and personal, something that came along without permission and demanded attention, demanded the energy of the artist be exerted in an unexpected way. What was once concealed was now in view, exposed, and, in the sense that potential masks had been abruptly removed, whatever took place in the face of the disintegration of the devices used to demonstrate personalized skill, however the artist chose to deal with an unexpected systemic breakdown, for me, it seemed precipitously authentic. "Creativity comes from the freedom to fail, and the freedom to fail comes from experimentation, and that's what gives something its individuality" (Peter Gabriel reflecting on the work of Kate Bush, in Sibley).

Grappling with the sudden precipitation of authenticity is an art unto itself and so, unbeknownst to me, I was in for a treat when I attended one of the *Non-Linear* events, curated by Todd Anderson-Kunert and held at Strange Neighbour Gallery in Collingwood in the second half of 2015. Though they were scheduled to perform as a noise-drone duo, Piers Morgan and Ciarán Geoghegan's set ended up being Ciarán's solo with Piers on something more like a performance mime. For reasons never uncovered, despite a satisfactory sound check, Piers's gear made no sound whatsoever for the entire set—not a single squeak. He was clearly stressed, and understandably so, but, again, it was very interesting to watch what happens to the improvised music performer when the structures that support their presentation malfunction. A third example comes from the inaugural "Improv Idol," a mock-competition conceived and arranged by Clinton Green and Carmen Chan and held at the Wesley Anne in Northcote in 2015, "one part talent show, one part music improvisation laboratory," during which Mat Blackwell also suffered total sonic failure (Green and Chan). Mat checked his gear and the audio engineer checked the cabling that connected it to the mixer, but neither of them could work out what the problem was.

Our conversation across the three-minute walk from the venue to my place was focused solely on the question of what went wrong. Only after we had arrived and were running some tests on his gear did we discover (quite quickly, actually) that, in this instance, the singe hindrance to Mat's, and possibly our, sonic pleasure was a single throw switch on his Korg Kaoss Pad that had mistakenly been left on the *line input* setting when it should have been switched to *microphone input*. I am not exaggerating when I say that, had Mat detected this detail while on stage it could have taken him less than thirty milliseconds to resolve the issue and continue on his quest for mock-music-stardom. Unfortunately, and his is by no means an isolated instance, in the heat of the moment, this simple factor slipped under the radar of anxious attention. Fortunately, Mat is remarkably inventive and not one to take himself too seriously, so it's not entirely surprising that he chose to engage his comedic disposition by crawling out of view beneath the crimson hem of a heavy stage curtain and remaining there for much of the set—with only the soles of his shoes visible—buzzing a jolly little tune on his kazoo.

Maybe I have chosen the long path to a simple point, that a person is defined not by the situation in which they find themselves but in how they choose to move through it, how creative resilience is exercised. For me, that is where the action and, therefore, where the artistic merit is to be found. This matters more than the timbre or composition of sound that might spill back into our ears once the audio-lines have been re-established. It is the kind of action I myself once faced head-on last in the first few minutes of a performance in which I participated as part of an experimental quartet. Our sound checks had been conducted without a hitch, yet, even as one of my fellow musicians stepped past me and asked "Are we ready to go, theoretically?" and even though I replied "yes, I sure am," in my mind I was thinking, "well, I certainly hope so." So, when we began to play and I realized that I wasn't sending any audio signals to the front of house mixer, the first thing I did was think back to this section of writing, back to the recollections I had detailed about watching my peers deal with unexpected on-stage failures, and knew it was as good a time as any to walk some of the talk I had been sharing. First of all, I went through the standard signal-line checks, making sure that the audio interface was being seen by the software, unplugging the USB cable and plugging it back into the laptop in order to retrigger, thus refresh, a connection between the two devices; nothing. I closed down the program and reopened it to see if that would work; nothing. I ran my eyes across all of the cables, making sure that everything was still connected properly, that I had not accidentally knocked a power supply out; nothing amiss. The strange thing was that I was receiving a pulse through my hardware sequencer from one of the other players, and I could see the visual feedback in my software confirming that the pulse was reaching its intended destination, but no sounds were being heard at my end of the line. I was getting a bit anxious about it all, and certainly self-conscious given that I was sitting there on the front of the stage, nestled behind an array of music-making objects but not making any audible contribution to the collective effort in any way. It was turning out to be a missed opportunity; I was letting everyone else down. The anxiety levels were intensifying, and I knew this wasn't going to help matters at all, but what else could I do? It was then that I remembered watching a short video on YouTube in which Buddhist teacher Gen Kelsang Dornying is talking about the importance of remaining calm under stressful situations. I attended a meditation day course at the *Kadampa Meditation Centre*, located in Melbourne's central business district, about fifteen months ago and found it incredibly helpful. Gen Kelsang Dornying was the main teacher for that course; he shared his knowledge of the benefits of mindfulness and meditation with compassion and good humor, and I have often found myself, whenever I can feel the pressure of a difficult situation growing, thinking back to that day and to the things he spoke about. If ever I cannot seem to recall his words clearly, if possible, I watch one or two of the few rare clips available online, and once again hear him ask: "Why should we have a thunderstorm because we are looking at another thunderstorm? It actually doesn't make sense" (Kadampa Melbourne).

This rhetorical question serves as an important reminder of how little good comes from allowing oneself to become entangled in another person's emotionality, or in the negative emotions we might feel arising in us when we are faced with a difficult situation. During a video made at a meditation retreat, Gen Kelsang Dornying quotes Geshe Kelsang Gyatso who, in his book *The New Eight Steps to Happiness*, says that "[w]hen we develop real patience our mind will be as stable as a mountain and as calm as the depths of an ocean" (New Kadampa Tradition).

This is the thought that came into my mind as I sat on the stage, now nearly five minutes into the set, still wondering what mysterious alchemy had been responsible for my previously functioning equipment to stop working. As I relaxed into the absurdity of the situation, as I started even to enjoy the humor of it all, something came to mind: I glanced down to my right where the sequencer sat on the old red carpet, its many blue LED lights blinking rhythms impotently in the half light, I reached over and flicked a little silver switch that controlled voltage output sent by the sequencer to the software on my laptop and heard a thunderclap of found sound rattle out of the PA, patterns of percussive metal clanging, adding to the extant cacophony of the soundscape. The sounds were familiar; they were mine—a constellation of sound snippets I had cut from recordings of my wedding ring being tapped against my stove-top were now bellowing into the ear canals of the audience members. There had never been a problem with my equipment. My sequencer, for example, was simply functioning in accordance with how I had decided to mess about with it; it had been functioning properly all along. It's just that this proper function was at odds with my expectations as to what the outcome should be. Yet, in taking a few moments to keep myself calm, sitting on the floor of the stage, I had somehow made enough space in my mind, enough of a hole in the potential for confusion and bewilderment and anxiety, for a potential solution to peek through. I had flicked a cognitive switch, then flicked an electrical switch, and now had my sound back, which in practice meant that I was able to carry on with the set. But, more than that, it meant that I was able to carry on with a positive feeling stemming from the knowledge that I had overcome the so-called problem. It was a single, meaningful glimpse into what Gen Kelsang Dornying says, paraphrasing Geshe Kelsang Gyatso:

> The most these external things can do is trigger the potential we already have to develop unpleasant feelings. . . . in the process of observing this, we start to gain some control over our mind. We start to realise, hang on, this isn't the end of the world. this is just a feeling; it will come and it will go, like a wave on the seafront; sometimes it ebbs, sometimes it flow, sometimes the feeling arises, and sometime is returns back to the vats space of my mind doing no damage whatsoever . . . in the process of observing this illusion-like feeling in the mind, whilst forgetting a little bit about we've thought was the problem, we come to know this inner peace. We [can] become so good at observing what our mind's doing and controlling our feelings, we become free. (New Kadampa Tradition)

As a contributor to the local experimental music scene, as someone who shares its appreciation for freedom through sound, I have always been its student; my first points of contact were made as a way of self-initiating what seemed like the most challenging writing task imaginable (i.e., writing about sounds I had never heard before). It is partly because of my experience as a watcher and performer of experimental music that I no longer feel as afraid as I once did of making mistakes and of having those errors seen by others, even when those others are people I do not know and who, therefore, cannot be ruled out as being individuals who would indulge in an impulse to announce their critical eye. I would rather pay attention to the issue of change, to the modulation of what was and to thinking about how that might be used to inform creative and interpersonal negotiations moving forward.

I have often thought of improvised music as an appropriate metaphor for life. More specifically, though, if we take this approach to the experimental music scene as a metaphor for the way that unexpected periods of intense stress can drive valuable learning, it is unsurprising to find the aforementioned dips into disintegration, to my mind, at various points over the past few months, as oblique precedents for overcoming adversity in the teaching environment.

We arrive, now, back at the classroom. In the last few days before beginning a new teaching semester, my timetable was changed. One of the units, for which I had been preparing, was one that I had been updating and delivering since my first day at the Academy at the end of July, 2011. It was a unit through which I had been able to define myself (or limit myself, depending on your expectations) within the institution and, while it was not the only unit I taught, it was inevitably one to which I had become intellectually and emotionally attached. Surely a teacher's sense of connectedness to a subject stands as a foundation stone of effective delivery. So, you can imagine what suddenly went coursing through my bloodstream upon discovering that in three days time I would be responsible for a final semester unit focusing on contemporary design issues, in which I would be required to critically assess, among other things, the visual communications output of nearly fifty emerging professionals—cortisol; lots and lots of cortisol.

There is a critique of skill here that deserves some attention, and for which I would like to refer to Paul Hegarty's chapter "Inept" in his book *Noise/Music: A History* (2008). Hegarty focuses on late modern music culture, in particular the punk movement and its antagonism to the technically skilled guitar-hero figure that played such a large role in commercial music in the late modern era. He (P. Hegarty 89) says:

> Years of polls for "best bass player of the year" and the like had consolidated a smugness among listeners and musicians alike that many found not only annoying, but a betrayal of music and youth. . . . The mainstream rock of the 1970s, whether progressive rock (now seen as regressive) or heavy rock, seemed to be predicated on an unbreakable elitism, based on virtuosity. . . .

> Many punk bands made a virtue of an actual lack of skill. . . . Ineptitude is a strong, fundamentally noisy anti-cultural statement. . . . The inept player will make many mistakes, or what are perceived as such. He or she will make choices and create combinations that are "wrong," and this is what has led to the belief in the creativity that comes from a lack of preconceptions and a willingness to try out anything, even if badly. The results can be taken (and in punk, were) as more authentic, the lack of preconceptions allowing a greater creativity and personal expression to emerge.

At the same time as they expose a historical challenge to creativity in the sonic arts, Hegarty's musicological insights also provide us with a critical framework for thinking about skillfulness and competition in other creative spaces such as the design-arts. Sounds and images are united in their complex relationship to consumer-capitalist culture and to the attitudes around skills that are applicable to their fields, and they are both multifarious creative arenas negotiated by individuals who seek a sense of authenticity in whatever it is that they do. The challenge to sound production that Hegarty talks about is likewise a challenge to creative visual production. Competitiveness in the design-arts cannot be denied; in fact, evidence of industry input remains the most important signifier of institutional relevance. In order for a school to seem worthwhile, it has to tell people, and they must believe what they are being told, that such and such an institution has precisely what the market requires—that, by buying the tertiary degree from such and such an institution, a graduate will enter the professional field with a competitive edge that will put them in good stead towards being successful in the marketplace. However much fun is had inside or outside of the classroom, it's this undercurrent of competition and status anxiety that keeps the whole business afloat, that lubricates the flow of income. But what it is saying is that future success can be secured by any student who enrolls in a course of study and becomes masterful in the rules and regulations of an existing design-arts landscape to which they, themselves, apply (using industry-standard digital platforms, editing programs, standardized resolutions and file formats to which all good work must adhere). Fine, but it doesn't actually sound very creative if we still agree with Taylor's definition of creativity as an activity "done not by rule, rote, or imitation, but with successful originality" and that, therefore, offers a path to true fulfillment (qtd. in Academy of Ideas). If skillfulness is the practice of rules, regulations, and routines, and if it denotes an expertise in, and ability to do, something, made possible through training, then I can understand the value of the industry-relevant design-arts graduate who can imitate the best of the best, who can meet expectations, fulfill the client's brief, and so help keep the whole system going.

5. Expert (Disciplines of Knowledge) — Part Two

> *Loathing of bias is the flipside of love of facts. Science, and many of the human sciences, are beautifully founded on evidence based, fact yielding work. The problem is that, in many of the most important aspects of existence, there simply are no facts available. The big questions that bedevil us individually and collectively have no facts to appeal to. . . . The hatred of bias reflects a longing for a world without a need for hard choices and the sacrifice these necessarily entail. We may well long to stick to the facts, but we eventually have to try to lead our lives according to values, which are inherently much more contentious and complicated structures. There is no merely fact-based road to a good and contented life.*
>
> — Alain de Botton

The underlying question I have been tackling does not have much to do with the intentions of any one particular education provider. Rather, my focus is on the challenges to creative authenticity that might arise when one's artistic output is entangled in corporate consumerism cultures. I appreciate the limitation that comes from my own disposition, as someone who has a stable enough job, who doesn't need to work full-time and so, at least for the time being, has the luxury of being able to pursue an arts practice of whatever form I choose without having to think about how it can be used to gain access to other people's money (i.e., how I can use my labor as a means to benefit indirectly from the labor of other people). This isn't to say that I would not be happy to sell my work, and let us not overlook the fact that the creative people to whom I made reference in the previous section, Other People's Stories, have all been very successful. Suffice to say, their work is not based upon commerce, and my interest in their work is driven by their form and content and not by their market value (the finer points of which I have never bothered to investigate). Rather, not having marketability or commercial viability as an outcome that is necessary to my day-to-day survival means that it isn't a driving force for my creative decision-making processes and, therefore, for the kind of work that I produce. However, we might question the authenticity of creative work that is built upon the invariant principle of commerce, at the very least, such work remains irrelevant to the aims and scope of a mystoriographical project.

This said, what I have presented so far is not the complete picture; it is difficult to quantify the valuable lessons I have learned from the students in my Contemporary Design Issues (CDI) classes—third year Bachelor of design-arts students whose last semester of study has included taking guidance from me within a unit I have never taught before. As is usually the case when we find ourselves in unfamiliar waters, as well as taking responsibility for the learning outcomes of the unit, there have been times when I have also felt like a student. But what have I been learning? How does this learning feed back into an attempt to expose and articulate my invariant principle? Let's begin with the broad brushstrokes, and access details pertaining to the very observation from which change has resulted.

The CDI unit is designed to help students engage directly in some of the key issues relating to contemporary design and designers, such as sustainability, ethics, social design, design as a philosophy, design as a weapon. They are supported in the development of their independent judgements relating to the functions and implications of various design projects, to discuss and debate design issues within a social and cultural context. The unit requires students to choose a contemporary design issue that interests them. They are asked to conduct preliminary research that will help them clarify the focus of their study and, once this clarity has been achieved, each student must conduct an interview with a design-related professional from whom further insight into that insight can be gained. It is an expectation of the unit that each student develops a creative outcome that responds to the design issue in some way that facilitates public awareness around it.

In my role as a facilitator of their self-directed learning, rather than as some kind of knower-of-all-things who arrives simply to dump their knowledge and then leave, it has been greatly rewarding to see how invested students have been in their projects, to hear them speak about the things that concern them. One of the students has been pursuing her interest in the way that online behaviors are tracked by social media networks as a means to monetizing insight gleaned into consumer behavior.

There are many ways that this topic could be approached, from Bayesian belief networks, to which British filmmaker Adam Curtis brings our attention in the documentary *Hypernormalisation* (2016), to an article written by Hugh Mackay in *InPsych* magazine, the official bulletin of the *Australian Psychological Society Limited.* In Mackay's article "Softening us up for Surveillance," which focuses on the rise of reality TV, he states:

> In a society saturated by media—both mass and social—it was perhaps inevitable that we would come to regard mediated information as being in some strange way superior to the flesh-and-blood, three-dimensional variety. . . . "Reality" media have been conditioning us, however unintentionally, to accept and even to welcome the idea of a camera being trained on us — whether our own or someone else's. (23)

I gave a photocopy of this article to my student yesterday, by which time she had already been looking into the issue of ad tracking and targeted advertising. As part of her creative research process, she was required to select an industry professional that related to her issue and conduct an interview based on the chosen topic. This interview could be conducted in person, via email, over the phone, or even on Skype. However, it was imperative that the student record the interview in some way (asking permission first), and reflect upon this information with a view to presenting an overview in the context of a short in-class presentation and in the form of a five-hundred-word written summary.

It turns out that the student conducted two interviews, during which she asked how the interviewees felt about the current state of the social media environment and what issues they thought were important for consumers of the online environment to bear in mind. Her first interview was with the representative of a company that focused on social media, online advertising, digital marketing strategy and analytics, and tracking. Her interviewee welcomed tracking, which is of little surprise given his professional position and income is at least in part dependent upon the widespread acceptance of targeted marketing and on the needs that other companies might have to engage third party groups that might provide them with statistical insight from which future corporate growth may be strategically planned. This representative was a clear proponent of targeted marketing and did not feel personally aggrieved by the capacity of Google, for example, to scan Gmail or of Facebook's capacity to access users' webcams. My student also interviewed an anonymous hacker and was excited to get a point of view from a professional who was in a more behind-the-scenes role, focusing less on the creation of content for companies wanting to capitalize on tracking and more on the economic, political, and personal implications for the general public. As a requirement of the unit, the student must use their research and interview data for the basis of their own creative response (i.e., an outcome that, in some way, helps raise awareness of the contemporary design-related issue).

Her preferred idea has been to produce a series of stickers that a person can use to cover up their webcam, with the image of an eye on it, for example. In this way, such a creative outcome would be both a reminder of the threat to privacy that exists in the face of highly sophisticated digital technology and the lay-persons limited comprehension of its remote machinations.

A different student chose to focus on the topic of imperfect fruit and vegetables, which speaks to the broader issue around ideals of beauty and how we evaluate the visuality of bodies deemed non-ideal. It is a project that could start all the way back with Plato's allegory of the cave and his claim to the existence of an aspatial and atemporal realm of ideal forms (of truth, justice, goodness, and beauty), tackling the problems of universals, all the way to the contemporary moment and representations of the body, specifically Sandi Yi's work in disability fashion or, a little bit into the past, Jeffrey Silverthorne's morgue photography that makes for poignant commentary on the beauty of the scar. We could also delve into the various esthetics of decay to which an ever expanding and international stock of urban exploration photography, videography, field recording, and writing is connected.

For this particular project, the student was interested by the environmental sustainability aspect of imperfect fruit, and I recall, during her presentation, how attentive she was to explaining clearly that Australian supermarkets are becoming so fussy when it comes to the produce they accept and reject that between twenty and forty percent of fruit and vegetables produced in the country are failing the cosmetic standards before they even get to the supermarkets.

The student drew our attention to an episode of the Australian series *War on Waste*, hosted by television and radio comedian Craig Reucassel, in which this very issue is addressed. As my student stated in her work for the class, the episode "shows hundreds and thousands of bananas being tossed away because they do not meet the supermarkets standards."

Supermarkets across Australia are becoming more and more picky when it comes to their fruit and vegetables (also discussed in Chang). Fruit and vegetables are being tossed away simply because they do not meet the cosmetic standard of the supermarket. It is estimated that between twenty and forty percent of fruit and vegetables grown in Australia is rejected even before it reaches the supermarket because the produce does not meet cosmetic standards (Dee, Cash, and Jackson). But what exactly are these cosmetic standards? A banana, for example, can be deemed too bent or too straight, too long or too short, too fat or too thin, and it is this level of fastidiousness that leads to forty percent of all bananas grown being thrown in the bin before reaching supermarkets, despite being entirely edible. We could see the students' passion for the topic; she was astounded by this seemingly irrational, institutionalized practice and concerned by the sheer magnitude of the waste it supported, and this visibility, this commitment, played a big part in the surprise and concern we experienced as members of her in-class audience; her energy inspired our energy. The student expressed empathy for what was wasted of the farmers and practices: their labor (and, by extension, their health), their time spent cultivating land, their consumption of a precious resource such as water, the pesticides folded into the soils, the harvest and collection of the produce grown, the third of all stock as it is rejected by the corporate buyer; when she expressed empathy it was clear from the various gasps and emotional vocalizations coming from the other students that we, too, felt sad at this multifarious system of loss.

For her creative outcome, the student has been considering the pros and cons of producing a one-off spoof catalogue containing only ugly fruit and giving her examples ugly names, while including information, alongside them, detailing the nutrients contained in them. Her aim for such an outcome would be to show the consumer the role that catalogues play in conditioning the attitudes and assumptions we take with us each time we go grocery shopping. We are what we eat, it is said. But there is much more to what we eat than its surface appearance. As it turns out, the student has decided to pursue an alternative idea she had been pondering—the idea of producing a poster campaign designed to highlight the radical alterations that ugly fruit would need to undergo in order to be transformed into esthetically pleasing objects (i.e., in order to be deemed edible). Specifically, the posters would mimic surgical procedure preparation images, showing us ugly fruit with various dash-marks drawn on them that identify blemishes or disfigurements requiring incision and clinical modification. This creative outcome option works well in the sense that it fosters an emotional connection to the issue in its audience by building upon a connection that is already part of the parlance of everyday discussion on personal appearance in the context of our internationally shared movements towards greater respect for racial and ethnic differences, differences in body type and physical presentation, differences in bodily ability, variances in intellectual capacity, in personal styling, and so the list goes on.

There is much more that the student had to say on this topic, including referencing the lists that Woolworths has available online for its suppliers and customers that outline the criteria each fruit must fulfill in order for it to be accepted for sale (more than ninety percent of every Granny Smith apple must be covered by green skin or else be deemed unsellable). As I listened to her speak about her chosen research area, it could not go unnoticed that she was authentic in her interest; she was genuine in her ambition to apply her design-arts training in such a way that she might actually be able to make some kind of difference to the thinking around fruit and vegetables to which the common consumer had been primed and accustomed. For me, it seemed as though she was, if in some oblique, indirect manner, expressing her creative and intellectual disposition. It is an honor to be employed in a role where one gets to listen to creative young men and women articulating their experiences of the world. The more I thought this, the more I realized that the previous students, and others, were experiencing a similar journey, a similar desire to find something meaningful to them that, through the generation and navigation of design thinking and through the translation of this thinking into the skill-sets of their discipline areas, they were seeking a level of authentic self-comprehension that they could take as a strength as they prepared for graduation from their degree program and, ultimately, that might help them in the future as they come into repeated contact with the challenges of professional activity.

This thought remained in my mind; the more I listened to the students' presentations, the more I could see how much their journey's resonated with the mystoriographical pathway, albeit an industry-centric and design-arts-driven cousin to Ulmer's personal-educational-professional triptych. I listened to a student who presented on the topic of photography and the democratization of technology, in which he talked about how improvement in the capabilities and the accessibility of digital-visual technology has impacted on the social function and status of the professional photographer.

The student was concerned that, in a world where anyone can take high quality photographs, the specialist role of the photographer was at risk of obsolescence. I asked him what this notion of professional obsolescence meant to him; what really was at stake? We had a great conversation about how skill feeds self-identity and self-esteem and that, if the skills one possesses become less useful or special then maybe that poses a threat to one's ego. Could we understand the desire to protect the social status and exclusiveness of the photographer as a kind of elitism? Technologies advance in all sorts of fields: in medicine, in engineering, in mathematics, in information technology. The state of a society's play evolves constantly: the introduction of motorized transport meant the end of the horse and cart and its driver. So what if the value of what we had has changed or been lost? Revolutions in social awareness have led to the abolition of slavery and to the acknowledged rights of women to vote. So what if things are not how they were before? Moving forward has been unassailably positive. Apart from the self-esteem issue, so what if there are so many people with HD cameras at a wedding that there's no longer any inherent need to spend hundreds of dollars on a highly skilled photographer? At the heart of it, if we are to use the language of the times, that photographer is a *creative*, which for me means that they should be able to adapt themselves to whatever new conditions some to pass. If they are creative, then there must be some capacity to think on their feet, to imagine new possibilities for themselves and for their practice. For me, creativity is not about making and protecting a security blanket, but about building the kind of resilience that will see you moving forward in the field that you are passionate about even when you are suddenly faced with a blank page, with failure, with redundancy, with the bad weather that might seem to loom when our security disintegrates. Besides, perhaps there is too much focus on what technology is or is not doing to us, and not enough time spent thinking about our accountability in that technological picture. As Sir John Hegarty says:

> Just remember that no matter what piece of technology has been invented, from the camera to the computer, or will be invented, and no matter what value it claims to deliver, if it can't in some shape or another deliver the full impact of a well-told story its worth will eventually diminish. (49)

A few days had gone by and I asked this student how his project had developed since our last conversation. He explained that he was clear on the issue but was now experiencing creative block when it came to formulating a design outcome that addressed it in some way. First, I recommended that he speak with some of the other students in the CDI unit; a few of them had been dealing with the issue of creative block—a focus that, for two of those students, seemed like the logical outcome of their own inability to think of what to do their project on. But then, I remembered something else I had read in Sir John Hegarty's book, relating to the way that routine hinders creativity, and so I grabbed the book out of my bag, opened it up to that passage, and read it to him:

> All too often in your creative life you will find yourself stuck. You'll be beating your brains out trying to think of something different but despite your best efforts nothing is happening. Inspiration will not strike. Well, there's nothing unusual about this situation, so don't panic. I've found there's one simple trick you can use that will get you out of any creative rut. Swap seats. (J. Hegarty 112)

It's good advice, and I expect that there are numerous situations in which seat swapping can be enacted as a tactic for prompting creative thinking. However, I suggested to my student that he mix up the formula in some way. Where he had been focusing on highly advanced technology and how it would seem that people need less and less skill to arrive at an esthetically pleasing product, why not turn his attention to incredibly primitive photographic technology and somehow use it to communicate a message about what it really means to be a photographer (i.e., the skills that might carry one through multiple changes in the apparatuses one uses, story-telling, composition, quick thinking, curiosity). Would it not be compelling to articulate these qualities and values through something as out-dated as a pin-hole camera. Could it be that, by making and using a pin-hole camera, the student might return to those underlying principles and produce images that he could leave blank or into which he could incorporate a slogan of some kind to crystalize and press the point he wishes to make? The student was visibly energized by this new prospect, even though he had never heard of a pin-hole camera before. I expect that there are many soon-to-be-graduating photography students who have never heard of a pin-hole camera, and no wonder; we live in a culture that demands immediate gratification, and we are accustomed to constantly looking toward what is next; our relationship to history is ever challenged by a quasi-futurist techno-fetishism. In an age of Google Glasses, who bothers to go shopping for a black-and-white television set? The important thing was that the student immediately did an online search for information on the pin-hole camera and laughed out loud upon learning that he could probably make one out of a shoe-box.

These kinds of transformative moments are what have made this semester quite amazing. One of the other students started her research project learning about the psychology of waiting, specifically the waiting required en masse at the Etihad stadium—a location she's very familiar with. In the weeks leading up to the AFL (Australian Football League) Grand Finals, which saw her favorite team (the Richmond Tigers) go home with their first Premiership win in thirty-seven years, hers was a topic or incredible relevance. But, as she ventured further into it, the focus mutated, somewhat, and she became increasingly interested in the idea of procrastination. The things was, she also came up against a mental roadblock and also came to me for advice on how she might get over it, or around it, or even through it. With Sir John Hegarty's *swap seats* concept still in mind, and given how it helped the photography students to at least start thinking again about their project, it made sense to share this tactic with this other student who now needed my help. I asked her to talk me through the ideas that she had thought about producing, requesting additional information relating to why they had ultimately seemed insufficient. At least that way, by showing me the things she has pushed out of view, metaphorically speaking, maybe then we could get a sense of the shape of the clearing that now existed in front of her. As she talked, I kept hearing her explaining different ways that she might visually communicate the disadvantages of procrastination. The more I listened, the more I wondered why she was so caught up on the negatives and asked whether she thought that showcasing the positive aspects of procrastination might be a worthwhile path to take. It would certainly remain coherent with her initial research focus, which was about understanding how people could be encouraged to accept waiting, how we could embrace delayed gratification in a healthy way, how we could learn to be more patient. In my mind's eye I could see a series of posters promoting procrastination and what critical contrast they might bring if displayed in the context of a tertiary design-arts institution, on the walls alongside that institution's own posters that promote skill and efficiency and productivity and all of the things that it knows the industries, upon which its educational relevance wholeheartedly relies, themselves value. What better way to re-energise the understanding of institutional consensus than by offering an alternative position? What better way to demonstrate the industry-specificity of one's critical thinking than by being constructively critical of the very rooms in which you are breathing now? It was a thrilling mental image, which I shared with the student because it seemed like a useful opportunity to foster her own design thinking beyond the box that she said created for herself. She will be graduating in just a few weeks; finding ways to break out of the box is precisely what she is imminently considering. In the end, this student produced a poster in the Soviet style but with her own sense of humor injected into the message. The poster has a yellow background with a picture of a closed fist in black outline, directed upwards, positioned in the center. Above the fist are the words "Procrastinators Unite!" and, below it: ". . . Tomorrow." It offered a poignant reminder of the personal hurdles that even collective effort may not overcome, a reminder of the apparent emptiness of ideological slogans when they are seen in the face of a material reality, as well as evidence of the positive outcomes that can come from being honest about unflattering stories.

This is the point where I realized first-hand that I'd been focusing on the wrong side of the industrial and institutional fence; in the course of my discussion on the professional domain of discourse that informs my invariant principle, in my previous expressions of concern that the capitalist co-option of the skills of creative young people somehow posed a great threat to their authenticity as cultural communicators, because they would likely end up producing acts of visual communication designed to convince people to buy things they didn't need. I had been focusing on the competitive use of creative skill for profit, for the reproduction of a capitalist culture, away from art as David Mabb sees it, and towards alienated labor.

In many ways, the rhymes and rhythms of our daily lives are still conditioned and controlled by the profit-driven demands of capitalists, thus we remain vulnerable to exploitation. Wherever we might find exceptions to this rule, though even not-for-profit organizations must wrangle with the conflicting pressure placed upon them by big business and its allied government, what we can claim with unwavering certainty is that the commercial design-arts sector is not one of these exceptions, and we thus know that any institution constructed with the express purpose of preparing creative young minds for their long-term integration into these spaces is explicitly implicated in the grooming of hopeful individuals who pay top dollar for institutional guidance for later exploitation.

For me, then, the idea of designing for a capitalist culture has always struck me as a formalized and normalized betrayal of creative potential. What I overlooked, which perhaps is not the only thing, was this: just as my students enter the class room as whole people whose personal lives, ideological positions, socio-economic circumstances, psychological strengths, and vulnerabilities all impact on how they conduct themselves within it, just as their academic and practical abilities could never articulate their self-identities, so too does it make sense to think these emerging professionals will eventually carry their wholeness into the design workshop, studio, or office, however much of it remains unseen. In her role as a guest speaker promoting the role of the *Communications Council* and, in particular, the function of the councils twelve-week *Award School* internship program, Suzy Leys stated that they put most of the recent graduates with whom they come into contact into public relations roles; rarely do they get to go straight into creative activities for which they have been trained. Graduates can tell, for themselves, whether this opportunity is suitable to their needs. However, regardless of any pressures that might be placed upon graduates, any authenticity they take to the table must surely remain within them as potential, as dispositif, as creative disposition, as an expression of their invariant principle, even when dealing with difficult situations or with difficult people. Ethically speaking, you can only take what is already on offer; who am I to pass judgement on what the details of that offer should be? Who am I to say that they will simply apply their efforts to the reproduction of what already exists. So long as the students go on to look for positions where they will be respected for the empathic and vibration thinkers that I have clearly seen them to be, what could be the harm in that? It's less about skill and more about the capacity to demonstrate personal choice in an ethical and sustainable manner.

Perhaps there is something to be said of this as a testament to the value of taking the heavy-handed, veritably scenic approach to a mystoriogaphical experiment, as opposed to the fleeting, cursory, Nietzschean-esque *lightness-of-touch* approach of which Ulmer has spoken. The gently, gently style is appropriate for students and the time poor; for me (someone who has the luxury of time—the capacity to make time across my weeks—and the predilection for language-based self-interrogation), the prolonged, in-depth approach gives me the germination time I need.

In my mind, it was the privileging of skill that facilitated a creative worker's labor value, which therefore opened up the vulnerability to capitalist exploitation, that underpinned my ongoing suspicion of skill in general and in the industrialization of creativity in particular, in the competitive application of creativity for profit because, as Marx theorized, whoever holds the profit also holds the torch of exploitation, who now enjoys its affects and who, therefore, puts workers further to task in an attempt to see to it that this enjoyment continues.

But, here is a convergence of form and content that is not inevitable. Let us think back to Kate Bush who danced a most unusual dance to a song about a book, a song she wrote as a teenager, and yet she made it commercially available. What is the image of my three-year-old-self dancing to "Wuthering Heights" with a long piece of toilet paper being flapped around by my hand, but an image of a body moving freely in a box (commonly known as the lounge room), watching a body in a dress dancing freely in an illusion of boundlessness contained inside a box (identified as the television set). Freedom in a box—freedom packaged in a manner that rendered it transmittable to others and enabled it, as it did for me, to become a facilitator of other feelings of freedom and maybe make such an impact (tacit proof of its effectiveness) that I, the viewer, nearly four decades later, cites it as a significant factor in the course of my creative trajectory—a key domain of discourse from which my invariant principle has been articulated.

Perhaps we can also think of this in terms of a babushka box of creativity. Fluid, seemingly improvisational movement taking place amid structure—supported by it, showcased through it. This lounge-room scene from long ago represents a multi-tiered dialectic between freedom and constraint, reminding me of the *OuLiPo* (*Ouvrir de Littérature Potentielle*, or Workshop of Potential Literature)—a post-WW1 group of French writers and mathematicians, but the sentiment can be applied to all creative language forms whose motto offered a mascot for new literature. As the group's co-founder, Raymond Queneau, put it: Oulipians are "Rats who build the labyrinth from which they will try to escape." Yet, to run away would be to miss the point.

Perhaps creative authenticity is less important than commercial success gained through competitive behavior. The *Concise Oxford Thesaurus* associates *competitiveness* with aggression, opposition, and ambition (aspiring for success—denoted by an ambition to win some, or all, of the prizes), which shows competitiveness to be rather at odds with humanitarianism (fellow-feeling, magnanimity) (Kirkpatrick 129, 374). Thus, if we take Paul Hegarty's aforementioned incredulity towards *best player polls* and their various manifestations as indiscriminating (the problem is not with music per se but with an aspect of mainstream music culture that privileges specific rules of engagement), perhaps we may also suspect that competitiveness in the design-arts (as a commercial, popular endeavor propagated via mass media) consolidates a smugness among professionals and students alike; irrespective of whether or not we find it annoying, perhaps the reader will worry, as I do, that this undercurrent of skills-based competitiveness (that systematically pits students against each other and, in turn, alienates them from each other) amounts to a betrayal of creativity and youth.

Nothing levels the playing field like something going horribly wrong. In the case of things going wrong on stage, it's in the aforementioned kinds of stress-inducing moments, of which I have experienced one or two myself, that a person's self-identity as a creative human is put to task, laid bare, as it were, as an authentic self-presentation to the audience. Life is not a streamlined confluence of picture-perfect moments; it is full of errors. The messiness of life is one of the things that unite us (like the dust that gathers on a gold-plated mantelpiece, mess does not discriminate). So, whatever story my field of professional expertise tells about itself, when it comes to capturing meaningful feedback regarding people's experiences, I think that there are more useful things to take into account than who is the best, ever, ever, everest. I am guided forward by my physical and intellectual investment in the experimental and improvisational music scene here in Melbourne when I reflect on my work-life and say that I want to hear about the person (from the person) who careened off of the road and drove into a ditch (unless it's Filippo Marinetti, or the toad of toad hall—a fictional character featured in Kenneth Grahame's 1908 novel *The Wind in the Willows*, both of which seem to me to wave the flag of mechaphilia and run the very real risk of road-side trauma). There is value in the ditch diggers' stories—the wobbly ones, the stories of the students who are not competitive in their chosen fields and so experience difficulty finding sufficient employment. There is value in stories about what went in a direction that isn't ideal. Just as these are stories of trying and struggling and not quite getting it right (stories about learning), it is from these stories that those who are positioned as *knowers* might actually learn something new and, through that learning, prioritize honesty (have courage in fallibility) with regard to whatever creative practice they pursue—whether together or in isolation, or via permutations of the vague and shifting spaces in between, where one state will tip into another.

6. Formulating an Invariant Principle

> *I'm not entirely sure that I am able to make sense out of whatever I come across, at all, except in the effort of recording it. So, whatever sense there is, is primarily an aesthetic sense and I realise, you know, that making in prose a decent pattern out of what happens to come your way is a preoccupation which, in a sense, has no higher ambitions, really, than for a brief moment in time to rescue something out of that stream of history that keeps rushing past.*
>
> — W. G. Sebald

It is useful to return to the interrogative (3-question) structure that Ulmer provides, but to do so in a non-linear way, so as to respect the unfolding connections between the three discursive domains encapsulated in the mystoriographical triad.

5a. How does the world work? What is reality? What one of the narratives tells us about the answer to this question? To question the nature of existence and of what it means *to be* is to pose an *ontological* question. The term *ontology* stems from two Greek words: *ontos* (being, to be), and *logia* (the study of, the theory of), and so refers to "The science or study of being; that part of metaphysics which relates to the nature or essence of being or existence" ("Ontology" 2001). So, when Ulmer invites us to consider how the world works (when he prompts us to question what reality is), he is asking us to make an ontological consideration, an evaluation relative to our own experience of the conditions of existence. Ulmer extends this invitation because part of the meaningfulness of the mystory comes from our decision-making around how one of the three narratives reflects the nature of reality. In other words, what ontological theme or insight can be seen to underpin one section of the mystory?

By choosing to take the personal memory of the invisible thread in the school-yard as the subject of my ontological question, it becomes my task to identity what can be known about the meaningfulness of social existence (i.e., what it means to be a human in proximity to other people). There is a dilemma at play in that I am unable to interpolate a statement about the world based on just my own experience (always a problem when the sample size $n = 1$), particularly if it comes to pass that my own experience is abnormal. Though, I am not claiming to be speaking for anyone else, nor do I require the agreement of others as to my *Weltshauung*, my own *world-view*, based upon my own experiences. Furthermore, what is wrong with a little idiosyncrasy; is not idiosyncrasy precisely what the mystory seeks? Normal or otherwise, my experiences exist as part of the broader field of detail to which I assign causality (making assumptions about why certain personal experiences have come to be) and upon reflection of which I characterize the ontological position that underpins my own creative disposition (in view of which I use creative languages).

This is my worldview: being alive means having to negotiate emotional ties to an unfathomable past.

5b. How do I feel about it? What is the mood in which I undertake these actions in the world? What is the attitude, the esthetic? This question of mood and feeling, of attitude, prompts us to make an epistemological consideration. The term *epistemology* comes from the Greek words: *episteme* (knowledge, understanding), and *logia* (the study of, the theory of), and so refers to "The branch of philosophy that deals with the varieties, grounds, and validity of knowledge" ("Epistemology" 838). Thus, if we are thinking about the attitude with which something is undertaken, what we want to clarify is the basis of understanding in view of which that thing is done. As David James says: "There is a relationship between theory and practice [thinking and acting] that implies an epistemological position." What is presumed to be true for such and such an action to be understood as meaningful in some way? Because this mystory project is based on a relativist ontology, of course it entails an interactive, personalized rendering of the information gathered. The self cannot be objectively approached, nor need it be; the meanings discovered are drawn from an in-depth and nuanced understanding of what has happened and are always kept in view of their context. Knowledge of my invariant principle, specifically how I go about esthetic activity, is based on this emic approach (truth is created by meanings and experience and not pre-determined).

For this section of the mystory, I am choosing to focus on my memory of dancing to "Wuthering Heights." What knowledge can be ascertained from inside (through close engagement with) the researched realm? As aforementioned, two video-versions of "Wuthering Heights" were produced; curiously enough, despite my living in England when the song was released, a great majority of my viewings have been of the US version. This is because, even though I have carried my love of the song across the years, it has only been since YouTube was established that I have had the opportunity to watch the video again. In the meantime, I had forgotten what the video looked like and so, one day when I first happened upon the US version, I simply took this as being the only version; I didn't know that there was an alternative video. I was an adult in Australia watching the American version of an English song I'd first heard thirty years prior. Little did I know I was watching the "wrong" one, so to speak, and watching it many times. It has only been in the past week that I (re)discovered that the white dress version even existed—the dancing in the void space version is most certainly the one I would have first encountered on the television screen located in the corner of my English lounge room at the time of the song's release—further proof that the human memory, at least my own, is unreliable.

In relation to the red dress version, on the afternoon of Saturday July 15th, I was driving home from Brunswick Street with my wife and daughter, a journey that takes us along St Georges Road through North Fitzroy and past the west side of Edinburgh Gardens, a large reserve popular with the locals, who pack it with picnic rugs and cider bottles on public holidays. While driving past, we saw dozens of men, women and children wearing red dresses; they had gathered together for another instalment of "The Most Wuthering Heights Day Ever," an annual event where Kate Bush fans recreate the "Wuthering Heights" video. The event, the Melbourne leg of which was organized by Katherine Brandenberger and attracted more than two thousand participants when it was first held here last year, on the same day was hosted in fifteen other cities around the world including Sydney, Tel Aviv, Montreal, Atlanta and Amsterdam (Webb). It was a light-hearted opportunity to dance with a big group of people, but it was not immune to the question: why was there not a white dress to be seen? Why was it only the US version of the video clip that was being re-enacted? Why not the UK version, which was, after all, the original version specific to Kate Bush's country of origin? For me, and certainly in the context of this discussion, given my focus on the *white dress* version of the video, the event was less a tribute to Kate Bush than it was a testament to the dominance of US-centric entertainment media. I thought perhaps the black and white versus color video had had something to do with the public's accessibility to color television. However, in 1978, many television programs were being broadcast in color, meaning that technological conditions in the United Kingdom did not necessitate the production of black-and-white or low-color tele-visual media. Furthermore, UK consumers had been buying color sets since the late 1960s. "Colour TV licences were introduced on January 1, 1968, costing £10—twice the price of the standard £5 black-and-white TV licence" and, by 1976, color television sets outnumbered black-and-white sets (Baird). The United States was introduced to color television in 1950.

Whether we are referring to the UK version or the US version of the "Wuthering Heights" video clip, in both instances a decision has been made on behalf of the viewer—the three-year old. Now, as an adult whose capacity to demonstrate personal choice is greater, it makes sense to wonder what implications there might be for the mystory if, through a paradigm test, the semiotic signs found in the UK video-as-text were substituted for those found in the US text. The sign-choices made in the meaningful construction of any text, including each "Wuthering Heights" video, alert the viewer to its ideological point of view as well as its limitations, and it's this insight to which the epistemological question is directed—what does the video seem to know/assume and thus present as worth knowing? What might be the grounds of understanding by which the creative act is approached/performed? The dance routine presented in each video is mostly the same, but how might the meaning of the presentation change if we swap a white dress for a red one?

In the US version of the "Wuthering Heights" video clip, the white dress can be said to signify purity, thus it stands as a metaphor for essence. Even so, this is not the case in the red dress version. Here, there is no abyss of Being that grounds the performance, but a green field dotted with trees. We are in the garden now, perhaps an Eden, with no-one else around apart from the unseen camera-person. The red dress connotes sexuality, like the famous dress worn by Marilyn Monroe or the dress worn by Kelly Le Brock in Gene Wilder's film *The Woman in Red* (1984) or even *The Lady in Red* (1986) by Chris de Burgh. There has been a scientific study into what is now called the *red dress effect*: psychology researchers from the University of Rochester, USA, and the University of Innsbruck, Austria "found that men who were shown photographs of women wearing a red shirt found them more attractive compared to when they saw the same women wearing green or white garments" (qtd. in Gray).

How might my epistemological awareness differ if we take away the void space (the apparent absence of a fundament) and replace it with a rural landscape (with earth, with literal foundation)? Perhaps I would not be so curious about notions of the abyss, such as Martin Heidegger's understanding that:

> Being is *Grund* and remains without any ulterior foundation: "Being 'is' the *Ab-grund* inasmuch as Being and *Grund* are the same. For Being 'is' to found [gründen], and only for this reason Being has no other *Grund*." . . . Being is therefore foundation, but in its essential form is by now only abyss. There is no contradiction, because the essence of Being, i.e., *Grund*, is not in its turn a *Grund*, but something like an abyssal intensification. (qtd. in Cristin 47)

Heidegger's ontology resonates visually with Kate Bush's white dress version of "Wuthering Heights." Even though we are now concerned with an epistemological question, this Being-ness of the abyss is still useful. If the abyss can be identified as the groundless ground of Being, then it must also provide grounds, however paradoxically, for whatever knowledge (produced through worldly experience) is presumed to be true. For me, it seems that creativity somehow facilitates the negotiation of a personal abyss (we may reconnect with our nuanced worldview, and psychological landscape, albeit by way of parallax, through the rituals of arts-related practice, perhaps as a means by which to reset and energize ourselves). We may, therefore, refer to art practice as a model of behavior that refracts and reverberates through other of our worldly activities. Put into its material context, a void space provides the backdrop for Kate Bush as she dances freely like a transient apparition or lost soul, singing a song about a book. Against the backdrop of this encounter with the abyss, what is worth knowing about creativity?

This is my epistemology: creative practice gives articulation to personal freedom (i.e., demonstrates, evidences, and proves freedom; practice feeds back renditions, representations, distortions of autonomy).

5c. Consult the mystoriographical pattern to answer the question "what is your morality?" How should I behave in light of this apparent world-working?

> *Human freedom is an ability. It is the unique ability, made possible by a first-person perspective, to reflect on and evaluate our desires and to choose one course of action over another. Only those with such an ability can be morally responsible for what they do.*
>
> — Lynne Rudder Baker

The word morality is defined as the "doctrine or branch of knowledge that deals with right and wrong conduct and with duty and responsibility" ("Morality" 1827). Morality carries connotations of goodness, virtue, principle, and integrity. It connotes honesty (as does authenticity) and is manifest in principles of behavior.

John Locke, one of the most influential Enlightenment thinkers, said: "We are like chameleons, we take our hue and the color of our moral character, from those who are around us." This claim is grounded in Locke's concept of the *tabula rasa*—his behaviorist argument that we are born as a kind of *clean slate* or *blank canvas,* that our knowledge of the world is gained through our experiences of it—through trial and error and not through pre-destined disposition. Drawing again from Sir John Hegarty, the blankness of the canvas can be addressed, first, with some small sketches, in which a plot or personal character might be little more than a few discrete marks that will gradually evolve into a whole picture. Likewise, a whole novel isn't in your head before you start to write. A plot maybe, a character. Well, write those down and gradually a picture will emerge, the story will begin to unfold.

Implicit here is the social constructionist perspective that creative individuals are produced by the circumstances of their lives and not born with talent already installed. It accompanies the now well-established view that culture is a construction and not invulnerable to renegotiation. This has had profound implications for queer theories, for women's rights, for class distinctions, racial identities, or any other branch of knowledge that engages the nature/nurture debate. In relation to the design-arts specifically, however, Locke's work meant that for the first time in European culture it was possible to conceive of creativity, culture, and education as partners. If we consider that it is the people that we grow up with and the peers with whom we are surrounded who make us who we are, impacting in complex ways on our personality. Just as we are not alone in our achievements, so too are we implicated in any injustices that those around us perpetrate; in such times, our characters are also at stake (the term *peer-pressure* comes to mind), and, therefore, we are placed under an obligation to effect a moral, honest, and educational response.

So, what am I going to do about it? This part of Ulmer's mystory is a call to action, a call to deliberate, and the actions I have outlined in the professional domain pertain to experimental sound-art performances as critiques of skill, and to design-arts teaching (another kind of performance modality) in a tertiary institution wherein there can be found contrasting attitudes towards skilfulness. The challenge for me, therefore, is to filter through all that information, all those concerns, and freely choose to commit to a standard of behavior that speaks directly to the careering, perambulatory sensation of being alive.

This is my morality/method/ethical conduct: produce playful work that embraces nonlinearity, improvisation, perambulation, disorientation and distraction, dérives, and other notions relating to nomadicism (with scope to draw from my maternal Romani heritage). This could branch out into work about indeterminacy and careering, about human vulnerability (about loneliness, about lying awake in bed at night worrying), about how sounds articulate us—potential music discoverable in non-musical objects located throughout the built environment (sound-based urban exploration, the socially constructed voice and its fragmentation). Create alternative sonic perceptions of the city that defamiliarize and disorientate everyday life, sound walks that challenge the promise of visuality inherited from the enlightenment via the scientific imperative that *seeing is believing*, work that prompts recognition of oneself passing through networks of modulating and overlapping sound waves rather than simply walking through configurations of static architectural structures.

Creative output could take on the form of sound-art collage and experimental music, spoken word fragments, sound/language-based disorientations, field recordings.

3 A Brief Account of the Dominant Themes in my Creative Practice: 1992 — Present

"Mystory" is Ulmer's name for a mode of creative research appropriate to a postliterate age, one that would result in a multimedia text, such as a video or a performance, rather than a more traditional expository essay.

— Nathan Stucky, Cynthia Wimmer, and Richard Schechner

Ulmer's mystory opens with an image of wide scope for the creative practitioner's comprehension of the three primary domains of discourse that encode one's identity—the popular, the professional (also referred to as the *communal* and the *personal*). This project, which lends itself most immediately to the more traditional expository essay, has articulated these domains as they pertain to my own creative disposition, however excessively detailed or ruminative they may at times be, as a symptom of my pursuit of clarity. This is all part of the disposition with which I have become well acquainted over the years and, for the most part, fairly resolved. This mystory feeds directly into that sense of creative resolution, promoting mindfulness of it.

Michael S. Bowman and Ruth Laurion Bowman expect that a mystory will culminate in/lead to a multimodal creative outcome. Ulmer's aim is to facilitate creative activity of a species that speaks productively to the domains of its production, making for a reflexive creative pathway. If for no other reason than because our present techno-cultural circumstances are explicitly cross-disciplinary, the mystory should not end with its exposition, but rather leak ever outwards through its progeny. In other words, a mystory is not an end in itself but a fecund landscape on which many interesting specimens may be discovered, cultivated, harvested, and appreciated.

Nevertheless, for a time I worried that my embarking upon this process might be a redundant activity. Ulmer invites his students to produce a mystory over the course of a semester and, if they are anything like my students, are almost sure to be vivacious young adults in their late teens and early twenties staring headlong into the exciting front ends of their artistic trajectories, which I genuinely hope will be life-long in their duration, diversity, and reward. Then, how redundant might my engagement in this process be, given that I have been producing art, standing back and staring at it with tilted head and serious eyebrows for over quarter of a century? A critic might suspect that I would have produced enough creative work across that time period to be able to see, in review and with sufficient clarity, what my creative disposition is. I suppose my burning, self-critical and self-doubting question of the minute is whether or not this mystory is superfluous. Should I not already know the answer to the mystoriographical question?

For me, a mystory is an opportunity to look back over what I have done, to see the obvious that has, through its habituation, become oblivious. It is a chance to reflect and re-evaluate, reviewing the claims I have made of my artistic efforts, both in the context of the institutional critiques in which I have aimed for good grades, and as a recipient of informal peer feedback. It is an opportunity to think about my artistic statements and check, with the benefit of hindsight, whether I still believe they have been given in earnest, and therefore that I have acted authentically. Has the meaningfulness that I discerned in my past works at the time of their creation, a meaningfulness that I have tried to put into words upon their evaluation, survived to this day? Has my self-identification as an authentic artist itself been authentic? Perhaps I've been deluded.

It is never too late to learn, and Socrates's dictum about the unexamined life has no age restrictions. Let's not forget that Bill Viola was already in his thirties when he sat for the interview in which he, for the first time and thanks to his interviewer's comments, discovered something new about his art practice that, saw it (and thus himself at parallax) in a new way. Although, in retrospect, it all made perfect sense, for some reason this perhaps obvious detail had been absent from his mind's eye, oblivious. Already well into an artistic careering, Viola caught sight of an invariant principle that clarified, for him, the veracity and purposefulness of his creative perambulations. He still had something important to learn, as do we all; we are not Aristotle—the ancient Greek philosopher thought to have been the last person who knew everything that there was to know in his own time (Jeans 1093). I would also like to think back to what has passed, to see it again in a new light, and so it seems fitting to conduct some memory work of the key themes and traits of my creative work to date. Readers may discern for themselves whether or not my invariable disposition has been sufficiently steering the ship.

By far, the bulk of my artistic activity has been shaped by an obsession with lightless spaces or, at least, spaces in which discrete illuminations flicker and/or rest within sites or rooms of indiscernible geometry. It is unclear how much of this focus stems from my own tendency to be overwhelmed by too much sensory stimulus (over-bright shopping center lighting, for example), or by personal experiences such as my migration from England to Australia as a six and a half year old, from watching the UK version of Kate Bush's "Wuthering Heights" in which she performs in an apparently improvised way in a blackened studio environment, as if drawing imaginative lines in the air with her arms, her legs, and her glance. A certain amount of guess work is inevitable.

As an adult, I have had a lot of trouble sleeping at night, spending countless hours staring into the dark, thinking about things that had happened the day before, ruminating over happenings yet to occur, making up stories of possible albeit improbable eventualities, watching scenes from my distant past flickering like stage-plays of shadows on the walls of Plato's cave, responding emotionally to things that can't be changed, flinching at imaginary antagonists. Amidst all of the mental activity that the early hours of the morning seem to nurture, a lot of writing has been done, mentally, requiring no pen nor paper, nor the click-clacking sounds of the computer keyboard such as that against which I now tap my fingertips in a scramble to exorcize the last threads of thought from my mind before the day finally starts and the regiments of daytime activity spread their distractions out across the coffee counter.

Most recently, I have experienced trouble sleeping (often thinking about the progress of this mystory and whether or not I will be able to turn out a meaningful index), casting my somnolent and astigmatic gaze in the general direction of the ceiling, tracing hypnagogic pathways through what seem to me, between 2:00am and 4:30am at least, to be the dominant themes in my artwork since 1992.

By this time, I had already been studying photography and technical drawing at high school and enjoyed them immensely, not participating in a dedicated fine art class until shortly after my family moved to a seaside town in southern Western Australia, mid-way through my second-to-last year and as I approached the cusp of adulthood. I found this relocation incredibly alienating, but it was also an opportunity to make new decisions about who I wanted to be. Some traits changed, some remained the same, but it may explain why I soon revised my subjects and dedicated myself to art-making; it was through artistic activity that I was able to anchor myself materially, emotionally, and intellectually in an unfamiliar environment, to manufacture a custom interface for dealing with a material reality.

Due to my inexperience, I looked to the teacher for guidance and received approval when I began producing drawings based on photographs I had taken down at the Albany wharfs—along Emu Point. Before I earned my driver's license, my mother would drive me there and she'd follow me around the jetties as I took whole rolls of photographs on a manual-wind Kodak camera, including one image of a fisherman repairing his net, well-worn buoys in faded colors sitting in piles on a deck beside him, the bow and stern lines of boats knotted around steel, tie-down bollards anchored in cement, wooden pylons. I also took photos of various metal structures that must have made some kind of esthetic impression on me despite my ignorance as to their proper industrial function. Once the roll of film had been finished, sent away for developing, and then collected the next week (far different to the immediacy we have come to expect in today's digitalized society), I was able to look through the images of my first self-determined artistic subject matter and begin, what upon reflection now seems to me to be, a fairly mediocre series of corrosion-centric mindfulness drawings. Focussing on the interesting surfaces of things seemed like a viable artistic route for an amateur artist, such as I was at that time, to take given that I was not yet capable of producing creative work with any conceptual depth. I still have the prints in a postcard-sized display folder tucked away between rarely visited souvenirs of distant decades in a box in the back shed. I also still have the A3-sized art folder that I submitted at the end of my final secondary-school year, in which can be found some of the wharf photographs alongside the textural studies they inspired.

A year studying art and design at TAFE (Technical and Further Education) preceded my entry into an Associate Diploma in Fine Art (ADA). Officially, students needed to complete one year of this two-year course before they could qualify for acceptance into the Bachelor of Fine Arts Degree run at Edith Cowan University (receiving credit for their previous study enabled students to commence the second year of the Bachelors degree with everyone else). I had completed just six months of the ADA when my family decided to move back to England (this would turn out to be a very short-lived affair) and so, with special institutional consideration, I moved out of home and traveled four hundred kilometers back up to the city and went on to finish my degree.

The work I made throughout this time seems far less important to me now than it did back then, some of which involved pouring lots of white enamel paint and bitumen-paint and sealing the resulting complex patterns under thick layers of clear exterior varnish made by a company called Wattyl. I also went through a stage of layering paraffin wax that I would initially buy in 25 kilogram bags from a warehouse in a nearby suburb, carrying it all back in my arms, on foot and with a little bit of help from public transport, back to the university art-sheds because I couldn't afford a car. Over the coming days the wax would be gradually melted down in an electric frypan and applied to canvas pieces to create white-on-white textures (like unintentional, alkane tributes to Robert Rauschenberg paintings) with varying degrees of opacity. The work was esthetically interesting, but typically made with industrial materials.

Somewhere towards the end of my second year, I began experimenting with fluorescent light shone onto stretcher frames covered in dark-grey, almost black plastic bought from the local hardware store where it was kept in large rolls, continuing my predilection for trade-related art materials (by this time, I had gained possession of a trade-card that earned me modest but much-needed discounts). I'd buy a few meters, stretch the material over square wooden frames that I'd made and reinforced, and marvel at how the yellow light placed alongside an edge would create a purple reflection. This experiment came out of a very brief color theory lesson given by a sessional teacher; the main idea was that when you mix complimentary colors together (making what's called a *grey*), and then place one of those two original colors alongside the grey, the grey itself will somehow look like the complimentary color. For example, if you mix yellow and purple together, thus creating this new kind of grey, then place yellow next to that grey, the grey itself will appear purple. This was the basic principle behind my experiment with fluorescent light and plastic, and, though simple, I found it fascinating that color could somehow be visibly extracted, albeit through an optical effect, from a void space. In that same lesson, the teacher mentioned the Fremantle harbor, specifically the way that the tonal values of colors change when the sun has gone down and they are set against the darkness of the sky. It was only a very fleeting comment that she made, but it was enough to stick in my mind and lead me to the first of many night visits to the harbor.

I remember the fence designed to prevent people from climbing down into the structures of the dock. The first time I hoisted myself over it, I was terrified—less so of getting caught and receiving a fine than I was of getting hurt with no-one to help me. But, when I climbed down into the structure, in those adrenaline fuelled moments, I really learned to enjoy crouching precariously on the thick wooden beams beneath the boardwalk, a foot or so above the swelling black waters. I enjoyed the quiet solitude of that darkened space, unseen, watching the green, blue, and red lights of the distant dockyard machinery blinking and moving on a disappearing horizon. I felt as though I was balancing on the rim of a watery abyss, hanging onto a wooden beam with one hand while taking unsteady, long exposure photographs (some of which were thirty seconds long) with the single lens reflex camera I held in my other hand. As a result, many of the images I'd received back from processing had streaks of colored light in them, several lines echoing one another like a chorus of tildes.

This theme of lights dancing abstractly in the dark was the focus of my work for some time. What interested me was that the lights *danced* only in the context of the film negative itself; the lines were never present in the physical, visible space of the harbor. Rather, they were drawn onto the negative by virtue of whatever bodily movement I involuntarily made throughout the duration of the exposure (i.e., so long as the camera's shutter stayed open, drawing was done invisibly through the normal function of the technological apparatus). These lines were oblique inscriptions of my own bodily micro-performances in that intra-industrial context. The photographer is always implied in a photograph, because someone is releasing the shutter. But these perambulatory tildes, these colorful streaks on the photographic images that, in time, became the subject of the images, were proof of the human body, implying body awareness, endurance, balance, and exercise, and the same sorts of things that we have also heard Bruce Nauman citing when discussing his in-studio video pieces from the 1960s, such as *Playing a Note on the Violin While I Walk around the Studio* (1966), *Violin Tuned D.E.A.D.* (1969), *Stamping In The Studio* (1968), or, my favorite one of them all, *Walking in an Exaggerated Manner around the Perimeter of a Square* (1967). According to Paul Garcia, this latter work "represents a microcosm of the fundamental themes rooted in Bruce Nauman's colorful esthetic: circularity, repetition, minimalism, body awareness, and post-structural linguistic theory. These themes are ingrained into what is essentially a ten-minute performance of epic banality."

I was so invested in exploring the epic dances of ghostly light-effects that I spent an evening creating a real-time light-blur extravaganza, so to speak. According to the date written in permanent marker on a recently unboxed DVD-R that is now on the desk in front of me, it was on the evening of October 6, 2007, that I returned to the harbor. This time, I set up a tripod on the far corner of the main jetty, secured a mini-disc video camera to it, pressed record, grabbed the tripod's lateral rotation handle, and walked around in circles, non-stop and with as steady a pace as possible, for about twenty minutes.

Although the *harbor night lights* motif focused my practice for a while, the manner in which I documented the harbor environment evolved. I began experimenting with sensitive slide film (one of the Fuji Provia products). The images produced became reference material for installation artworks. For an installation called *MNI Set* (shown at the Perth Institute of Contemporary Arts, WA, *Hatched* group exhibition in June, 1997) I built three wooden boxes, 1200 millimeters (w) x 1200 millimeters (d) x 450 millimeters (h), and clad them in textured, silver and black metal sheeting (that I have since seen being used in the lifts of office blocks). Each had a floor built into it using a single sheet of galvanized steel positioned about 50 millimeters beneath the top, creating a very shallow trough. Each trough was sealed and positioned in the installation space. They were then filled with Palmolive original dish washing liquid, which is a bright green color. Directly above each trough, a power cable extended down from the ceiling with a UVA Light/blacklight bulb affixed to the end. Each cable stopped approximately 100 millimeters above the liquid pool. The room was blacked out so that the UVA bulbs (much less harmful than UVB) were the only light source, causing the fluorescent liquid pool to glow (the visitor sees a pool of phosphors). It was not possible to see that the trough was shallow. This format was re-visited elsewhere; people not realizing that the surface was liquid would be surprised when they touched the artwork with their fingers, or tried to use it as a seat.

Although the theme was consistent, I experimented with other box configurations and liquids, apart from an artwork included in a group show at the Moore's Building in Fremantle (WA), where I installed the same UV lights inside long wooden boxes (that I built and painted black) and then laid rectangular slabs of paraffin wax along their open tops. In a darkened room, it was very difficult to see that the boxes were there at all. A visitor walking in from the other brightly lit rooms, walked in to what appeared to be a series of floating, grave-like illuminations. It's only once the visitor's eyes adjusted to the low-level lighting that the black boxes supporting the wax slabs became noticeable. I had gauged a small cavity (like a miniature pool) in to the surface of a couple of the wax blocks and then filled them with blue food coloring. I recall an exhibition visitor telling me of his surprise when he touched the colors square and realized not only that it was not solid, but now there was evidence he had touched the artwork on his skin. Keen to exit the installation space, upon doing so, he got an additional surprise; now standing in a room with normal lighting, the stain on his hands was red.

For the duration of my undergraduate training in visual arts, I was a painting major who never actually painted anything (other than the wooden boxes I produced). It was only after I graduated from my Honors year that I began producing oil paintings, which were mainly two-dimensional interpretations of the installation work I had been doing up to that point (i.e., abstract, minimalist works in oils that involved heavy-handed use of dark blue washes to create deep-sea-looking compositions).

My artistic practice underwent significant re-evaluation during my PhD candidature. With the focus on writing, the practical side of things began to fade away. I was writing about historical notions of the abyss while learning about ancient Mesopotamian creation mythologies, for example, I created a genealogy of the metaphor of the *abyss* and then critically considered how the conventions for representing the abyss have informed contemporary creative practices, including my own. One of the struggles I had with this research project came from my understanding that, if the abyss is unfathomable, if it is inevitably beyond a person's faculties of determination, then any attempt to represent it can only ever be inadequate. What, then, is a representation of the abyss, other than a reflection of the artist? I kept thinking about Friedrich Nietzsche's idea that "He who fights monsters should look to it that he himself does not become a monster. And when you gaze long into an abyss the abyss also gazes into you" (*Beyond Good and Evil: Prelude to a Philosophy of the Future* 102). Postgraduate research projects require all kinds of long gazing and so, as the process went along, and as this thought played on high-rotation in my mind (as it has continued to do so), I began to reflect on my own apparent emptiness; the abyss became a metaphor for an indeterminable self. I began to think of it as a personal motif. In fact, despite all its imperfections, the whole project was about historical, cultural identifications with this idea, articulated through creative, visual modalities. I felt so close to this idea, that it's what I saw when, after the elation of graduation, I finally had a moment to sit down and consider the next step I might take and the kind of person I would need to be in order to take it.

To some, this might sound a little depressing, and I remember it as being a fairly positive experience. If we think about the aquatic abyss of ancient Mesopotamian creation mythologies (or the Black Sea deluge that scientists believe inspired them), then the abyss, while materially cataclysmic, is symbolically filled with great potential, like a prototype for John Locke's *tabula rasa*—the blank canvas that, at least in this case, is not an off-white linen color, but the blackest of blacks, primed to be filled. It also reminds me of the Kadampa Buddhist notion of the emptiness of mind as *clarity*: "Mind—That which is clarity and cognizes. Mind is clarity because it always lacks form and because it possesses the actual power to perceive objects. Mind cognizes because its function is to know or perceive objects" (Robsville). Self-identification with the abyss, from a non-Western perspective, accounts for a positive and perceptive state of mind—the kind of mind, we can understand, that is receptive to the phenomena of the word and predisposed to fathoming the patterns that worldly phenomena may form. Clarity of mind sounds to me like a fairly useful state of mind for a person to be in when embarking on a new creative project . . . such as a mystory.

Moving from Perth to Melbourne, at the end of 2008, resulted in a radical reduction in my living space. I no longer had a studio, and, while I still felt a desire to produce work of some kind, I had no sense of where to direct this energy. As a result, I wandered for hours every day trying to orientate myself to a new city, plus address the challenge I had set myself: if I am to self-identify as creative, how can I reconfigure my practice in light of my new material circumstances? This challenge was also an opportunity for the further reinvention of my creative identity.

Ever since my PhD, I pursued a writing practice as part of my creative activity. As I settled into a new life in Melbourne, I decided to focus on my writing and put it to what I thought was its ultimate test and exercise—attending experimental and improvised music gigs and trying to write about them. This led me to a period of time writing reviews for a local music press, but, more importantly, I started making friends with performers and, in time, joined them on stage.

I didn't need a studio to produce sound, and I didn't even need to make my own sounds. Today, I contribute to experimental music events held in and around Melbourne. My musical soundscapes are full of reverberations, which lends them to genres such as dark ambient and industrial. They articulate imaginary space. Of the many things I like to do sound-wise, I derive great joy from hitting metal springs and sending the audio signal through a mono-reverb, then a stereo delay, then a stereo reverb, and another stereo delay. This results in a saturated, deep sound wherein I have the ability to blend the reverbs in ways that results varying spatial fluctuations. When this effects chain is used to process vocals, it gives the impression of a person calling up to the surface from the bottom of a chasm or well, as if hopeful that any passer-by might stop to have a listen or, you never know, even call something back. It's what you might call an idiosyncratic attempt at interpersonal communication.

Additionally, over time, I have become increasingly interested in sounds found in the urban landscape. This interest has grown alongside my interest (developed out of my long walks) in urban exploration. Many of my recordings these days are made in underground spaces, wherein I have experienced first-hand how the ear, to borrow Lawrence English's (TEDx Talks) musings on campfires and cultural safety, allows us to "reach out into the black." An example of my output relating to this creative, cultural research interest, is the multi-modal exposition called "Intersections of Creative Praxis and Urban Exploration," published late 2015 in *The Journal for Artistic Research* (Issue 9). It discussed a range of esthetic, cultural, and ethical contexts of urban exploration pertaining to my investigative sound-based art practice (Prescott-Steed "Intersections of Creative Praxis and Urban Exploration"). The exposition included three audio files made in underground spaces and demonstrated my creative negotiation of them. One of these recordings was called "Walking Through a Stormwater Drain While Playing the Violin (1380 Returning Steps)." It entailed me setting my audio recorder down in a tunnel, pressing record, and playing a single note (open G string) repeatedly on my violin while walking down the tunnel and away from the device—further and further and further away. As I walked into the distance, the balance between the raw sound of my violin and the acoustic resonance created by the interior of the tunnel shifted, until the raw sound could no longer be heard, only the prolonged reverberations, which I understood to be the acoustic footprint, or signature, of the tunnel.

Another work, called "Ambient Urban Encounter," was included in *The Politics of Ambience*, an event organized by Sam Kidel and held at *Oxford Brookes University*, UK, in June 2016, that set "out to explore the political intentions and implications of projects that focus on ambience" (Kidel). My work was a field recording taken underground; the sounds of vehicles driving over man-holes and other road traffic sounds are audible in the background, transformed by the unique acoustic traits of the lightless space into which they bleed, oscillating the small bones in my middle ears and sending electrical signals to my brain. This sound work reflected my idea that, due to the legalities of these boundaries, we may interpret an encounter with the ambient sounds of subterranean space, at least in part, as an encounter with the politics of ambience. It uses sound as a way of giving people on the surface, whether listening in their homes, in their offices, or whilst traveling the kinds of public transport that can be heard in the background of the recorded soundscape itself, the opportunity to access the ambience of forbidden zones via parallax. The intention was that listeners might be prompted to think in a defamiliarized way about the urban soundscapes with which they are familiar and to which they contribute on a day-to-day basis. I suppose much recorded sound promotes this, though, given that recorded sound is always acousmatic (i.e., audible in the absence of its means of production, thus a sonic context of alienation). The contributions I made to the *Kinokophonography* artist collective between 2012–15 all belong to this broader foray into sonic realities—attempts to connect to the world (at least to the small segment of it that I inhabit) by being a student of sound; these attempts include the sounds of a Hills Hoist washing line being grazed with a saw and subsequently hacked apart, a recording of the faulty bearing on an escalator at the *National Gallery of Victoria*, the squelchy wetness of a worm farm, among other audio work. My contributions to *Clan Analogue* projects have reflected my utilization of found sound in an improvised, electronic musical performance context, accompanied by other musicians playing synthesizers and programming drum machines. Recently, I have had a sound work called "Language Has No Positive Terms" published by the Portugese journal *MATLIT: Materialities of Literature* (vol. 5, no. 1) in a special issue dedicated to exploring the voice as a medium for literature and the disturbances suffered by the medium caused by the combined effects of performance and technologies for mediation, representation, and reproduction"

I previously had a multi-media piece and a contextualizing essay, under the title "Feedback in a Looping System: Heuretic Pedagogy and Experimental Music," published through *Textshop Experiments*, which is an open source journal building on the work of theorist Gregory L. Ulmer, and through which I am fortunate to have had published several articles. I should not expect that these things will be as interesting to the reader as they are meaningful to me, so rather than spend too much time stepping through each of these examples, a third and final sound art-related detail, that I shall share here, is less a formalized artwork (so far, anyway), than it is a simple insight into my creative, sound-based approach to the urban environment. Although not a work in itself, it nevertheless speaks to the notions of perambulation, walking, and improvisation that are already evident in my work and, for this reason, is a glimpse of how I enjoy my freedom (off the clock) that may be useful in the broader wide-scope image in which my invariant principle may be discerned. Just outside the Northcote Town Hall, a short walk from where I live, there is a wooden power pole. Much like many others to be found across the urban landscape, this pole is reinforced at the base by several metal stakes. The stakes are spaced out, vertically, around the circumference of the pole and held tightly against it by a few rings of steel strapping approximately 2 cm wide and fastened at various heights. These straps are so high in tension that they produce a good-enough note when the lengths stretching between the stakes are plucked with the fingers or struck with a tent-peg, for example. Every now and then I'll stop for a moment to bang out a fairly convincing rendition of the intro to *Cursed Female*—a song included on the self-titled debut album of the now defunct alternative rock band Porno for Pyros. Music is potentially everywhere; it just needs to be creatively uncovered.

Although a portion of my practice now carries with it a range of ethical and legislative issues, there is cultural value to be gained from encountering alternative sonic perceptions of the city. Thinking more specifically about non-traditional contexts of the artist's studio, what are we to make of a studio that's two meters wide and 2 kilometers long with not an ounce of natural light? How does it relate to the temporal art-making space I inhabited nearly ten years prior—the structures under the harbor boardwalk? I have moved from images to sounds, from privileging the visual to foregrounding the sonic as the object of my investigative, experimental practice, without forgetting the allure of the lightless void as a space in which creative activity may occur.

My visual work was preoccupied with dark spaces, and now a number of my recordings have been produced in the subterranean cavities that we are prohibited to enter and yet upon which our living arrangements are immediately and intimately reliant (Melbourne is built on a plateau of solidified basalt lava; a sophisticated urban drainage system, comprising manmade pipes and cavities, which is required for directing stormwater runoff away from roads, roofs, pathways, and other impervious surfaces linking our homes, schools, and businesses). Visual experience is still important (torches are required for navigational and safety reasons), harking back to the Aristotelian "concept of a *sensus communis*, a coordinated (or deranged) 'community' of sensation in the individual" (Mitchell 77). Academy work (continuing on from the PhD) has been done concurrently with my evolving artistic practice: I have written about representations of the abyss in digital deep-sea imagery ("A New Frontier for Visual Culture: Thoughts on the Production and Consumption of Digital Deep-Sea Imagery"), about the abyss in film ("Nemo's Abyss: The Deferral of Undecidability"), about the representation of chaos in ancient Mesopotamian writing (the first writing and, therefore, the world's first written accounts of the abyss) ("Black Sea Abyss: Chaos and Writing in Ancient Mesopotamia"), about aleatoric and improvised music ("Improvising Everyday Life: The Performance of Practice-Led Research"), about conducting a dérive at what was then my university and place of employment ("Dérive and Defamiliarisation: Seeking Alternative Solutions Amid Institutional Architecture"), about the abyss and potential space in early childhood development ("Playing in the Abyss: Generating Potential Space"), about representations of walking in Norwegian black metal visual culture ("Frostbite on My Feet: Representations of Walking in Black Metal Visual Culture"), about taking my students on an excursion to the city where they embark on a treasure hunt for theory in practice ("Practical Theory: A Creative Approach to Design-Arts Education in Melbourne, Australia").

These and other of my writings all speak in some way to the perambulatory, to negotiating a sense of intellectual and physical place in space; they are psychogeographical and carry a wayfaring esthetic. They are about transgression, about walking into the unknown and seeing what is there. I cannot enter the abyss (if we recall Nietzsche's quote, the self harbors the abyss, with all the Tardis-like paradox that this thought elicits), yet I have written about it. I cannot afford the great sums of money needed to be part of a spectacular voyage to the deep-sea with people like director James Cameron and his scientist associates, yet I have written about the deep-sea on several occasions. All of this creative traveling has taken place through language—that sea of seemingly infinite possibility that promises the thrill of an adventure, and thus risk, described by Ferdinand de Saussure as "a system which has no positive terms, and by this he meant that signs have no special right to mean something in particular and not something else. Instead, signs acquire their potential meaninglessness by contrasting themselves with what they are not" (Bignell 9). Much like the language system upon which they have been launched, as if in some kind of unavoidable and implicit self-reflexivity (capable of providing commentary on the ontological spaces they inhabit), to varying extents my writings have remained in conversation with notions of surface and depth. All the while, Nietzsche's notion of the peering abyss has stuck in my head. Through language, I think I have tried to play with this notion, used language as a way to quietly (with little more than the clacking of the keyboard keys or the scratching of a pen on paper) participate in a game of the abyss, and used various abysses of the world, so to speak, as tools with which one might perform moves in a chess game. Because language is unstable, to speak of things beneath the surface, things found in the deepest of depths, of sitting in dark spaces and of trying to get lost in broad daylight, is to enjoy a kind of symbolic and psychogeographical destabilization.

Seeing how my writings relate is one thing. But what about my sound art? How does this fit into the image of wide scope? Thinking further about this, it is not so difficult to discern a link; I cannot afford to travel extensively around the world, but on a number of occasions I have sent my audio work across virtual space to people in the Netherlands, in England, in the US, in Poland, in Ireland, in Finland, consequently contributing to compilations or participating in new music events that I could never attend in person; my sound art submissions travel on my behalf. With these details, I do not look for credit, only patterns; it is through these creative avenues that I am able to make contact with the outside world, considering them now in an attempt to join the dots of the creative landscape that describes my invariant principle. For, however directly or indirectly my creative sonic and language-based activities pertain to a non-systematic, imaginative transgression of geo-cultural boundaries, they are facilitated and disseminated by the same thing—the internet. The internet is the manmade abyss of our digital age, seemingly boundless, and it is into this void that much of my textual and sonorific stuff' is released/flung/expelled, almost as if I were symbolically throwing myself into the depths with everything that I make and in a way that, now that I think of it, is reminiscent of Yves Klein *Saut dans le vide* (*Leap into the Void*) (1960), though without the photomontage magic. As I work on a soundscape of some kind, I do not see the Netherlands, England, Poland, Ireland, Finland, nor Maryland, and much of what exists around me in my physical environment is also blinkered out of view through an intense and prolonged focus on the task at hand; there is nothing to see before me but a glowing screen that connects me, virtually anyway, to the groundless void beyond, albeit one filled with binary data that extends into variable immensities far beyond the reach of mental faculties, and yet we know that they exist. The word *immensities* connotes vast realms of information that are discrete and linked and overlapping to such an extent that their boundaries are often hard to ascertain without such systematic mechanisms as fire walls, virtual flame gates that protect one data area from infiltration by other data areas. Virtual abysses have become the paradoxical landmarks of late modern culture; much like the excessive binary data streams that feed Ryoji Ikeda's immersive art installations, "we can't see them [these streams], but we know intellectually that they are there" (Herbert 164). In my case, I intellectually know that I have continued to return to the notion of the abyss in my creative practice, enacting a body of repetitions over time, executing rituals of the abyss so to speak, that have, in turn, anchored what I am now learning to call my personal metaphysics.

4 Assemblages: Towards a Sonic Psychogeography

For me, to get into that creative process I have to have a sort of quiet place that I work from, and if I was living the life of, you know, somebody in the industry as a pop star or whatever, it's too distracting. It's too to do with other people's perceptions of who you are, and what's important to me is to be a human being who has a soul and who hopefully has a sense of who they are, not who everybody else thinks you are.

— Kate Bush

Shortly before I began writing this text, I bought a four-hectare block of land just over an hour's drive north of Melbourne—on the south side of a quiet town in central Victoria called Heathcote, which is one of the gold rush towns that experienced a rapid influx of prospectors in the early colonial days. There is some interesting etymology at play here. The word *heath* means "(an area of) open uncultivated ground" ("Heath" 1207). It's etymological root, the word *heide*, is also the etymological root for the word *heathen*, meaning a "Gentile [pagan] woman. . . . inhabiting open country" ("Heathen" 1207).

Attending to the second half of the word, *cote* denotes a "cottage, a cot. . . . A light building or enclosure for sheltering or confining animals or for storing something; *spec.* a sheepfold" ("Cote" 522). I am reminded of Heathcliff—the man to whom the protagonist of Emily Brontë's *Wuthering Heights*, Cathy, speaks and, in turn, to whom Kate Bush calls in her song: "Heathcliff, it's me, your Cathy. I've come home. I'm so cold! Let me in-a-your window."

Cliff: "A steep rock face, now *esp.* one facing the sea. . . . A steep slope, a steep hillside" ("Cliff" 417). The fact of whether or not heathenry may be identified as the real recipient of Kate Bush's lyrics is not something that I am qualified to determine. Nevertheless, the etymological correspondence is striking—made even more acute whenever I have "Wuthering Heights" playing on high rotation in my mind, while I work on the land in Heathcote.

I can't help but wonder how much of an influence television shows like *Escape to the Country, Grand Designs* or the various forays into the tiny house movement (*Tiny House Big Living*) have had in my newfound weekend activity that comprises driving out here with my wife and daughter, to our twenty-one-square-meter wooden hut—a relatively light building in which I am presently sitting and writing under petrol-generator-powered light, listening to David Bowie's *Blackstar*, about which I have written for my first contribution to *Textshop Experiments*. Today was the fourth day that I have spent working with my father-in-law, who has been visiting from the other side of the country; he is a retired industrial architect, here helping his daughter and her husband with the construction of a thirty-square-meter deck for their little wooden hut in the country. It's a project far smaller than many that he has managed. Yet, as I listened to him explain each step of this modest building process, still, I could hear the depth of knowledge and the patience that I've always admired him for.

As I take a morning walk around the block, after a ten-hour sleep that sometimes seems possible only this far from city-centric distractions, noticing the various flora that grow on the surface of the rich red clay earth, the small feather-like weeds that span the gully and ripple like the ocean's surface when the wind brushes their tips, the papery yellow flowers, the unfamiliar species of wild-growing fungi that I try to cross-reference with the pictures in *Fungi Down Under* (Grey and Grey) an informative pocketbook I discovered recently at the *Centre for Education and Research in Environmental Strategies* (CERES) bookshop, which I knew would be useful on such occasions.

From the other side of the property, I look back over at the hut and see, as if exaggerating its scalability, not the new structure that now projects proudly outward from its weather-worn frontispiece, not the concrete-set stumps driven deep into the ground, but rather pylons used to support a harbor structure, not unlike the one million oak logs—sourced from the Schwartzwald several centuries before Nietzsche or Heidegger took long walks alone throughout its wild slopes—upon which Amsterdam historic buildings still infirmly sit.

What is a performance? Does building a 6 meter x 5 meter deck, fixing 24 posts to 4 bearers to 15 joists to 54 boards fixed down tightly with a total of 1620 decking screws, effectively spanning a generational gap count as a performance? How does the mental image of four adults hammering in concert, their arrhythmic percussive bursts ricocheting between the steep slopes of the hillsides, add to this appeal to the notion of practice—beyond affecting the kind of quasi-ritualistic percussion that might enliven a latent pioneering spirit? (I wish I'd had the presence of mind to make an audio recording.) Would it make any difference if I said that I had spent forty-five hours on it so far and that I had passed much of this time thinking about Ulmer's mystory and that this thinking had been regularly intercepted by the sounds of "Wuthering Heights" saturating cortical and sub-cortical network in my brain (admittedly not the whole song; mostly only the bridge and chorus—over and over again like an obsessive compulsion), wondering what artistic outcome I might realize that would have, embedded in it, an implicit confirmation of the value of the process, providing material justification.

I admit to being a little facetious here, but as long as we value flexible thinking, as long as we seek to initiate invention, the limits to our conventional classifications must remain vulnerable to playful (mis)behavior. Building a deck requires a plan of creative action; the word *dispositif*, as any French dictionary will show, means "device, system, plan of action" (Clari 55). Deck building is collaborative. The difference being, I suppose, that it has not been conducted in the context of a practice, has not been flagged as art and so does not necessitate critical cultural analysis, does not seek to facilitate conversation beyond that directly related to its own making (method, materials, the pleasure gained from reflecting back onto the fruits of shared manual labor, interpersonal relationship building, etc). This said, had I taken a video recording of the process, it might have been no less worthy of that ideologically loaded term *art* than Bruce Nauman's video *Setting a Good Corner* (1999) that, like many of Nauman's videos, seems to be *what it says on the box*, in this instance documenting

> Nauman's efforts to construct a fence on his American ranch. From a fixed position, the camera captures the artist engrossed

> in various activities, including digging holes, securing foundations and setting tension wires. In the closing frames, comments from his neighbours scroll, like end-credits across the screen, offering an ambiguous finish to the film. With its detached staging of mundane activity presented in an unending loop, Nauman's recording serves to reveal the laborious creative processes frequently hidden behind works of art. (National Galleries Scotland)

In the context of a creative practice, what creative project might I produce in response to the mystoriographical exercise I have undertaken that builds upon the insight I've gained through it? Could it be a video — with or without audio? An experimental found sound collage? What?

With all that has been said, it's difficult not to think once more about the UK version of Kate Bush's "Wuthering Heights" video clip and wonder if an improvised dance in potential space might be an impossibly hard act to follow. It should be noted, though, that Ulmer's creative research model has been conscientiously adapted for performance studies purposes, as per Michael S. Bowman and Ruth Laurion Bowman's paper *Performing the Mystory: A Textshop in Autoperformance*, in which they introduce the "Barthesian notion that every text contains a set of 'instructions' for making another text" and (as a "fundamental methodological principle in Ulmer's textshop") reflect critically upon its application to avant-garde writings and performances (Stucky, Wimmer and Schechner 166). Although my own work is not equivalent to the work of these authors' students, Bowman and Bowman's section on the evaluation of the mystory explains how

> many students that reported being "carried away" by the research component . . . of setting off on the trail of some more or less specific item, only to encounter along the way other equally interesting, though unforeseen, materials and experiences. . . . The textshop in autoperformance explores the possibility that the creative imagination is as educable as critical thinking and that the former facility may be as important as the latter in helping students locate themselves in the story of their community, family, region, or nation. (Stucky, Wimmer and Schechner 172–73)

For now, throughout the course of this mystory, a key thing I have remembered is, on a macro level, just how much of a role the abyss metaphor has had in how I make sense of everyday life (the language paradigm is use in order to articulate self-identity in a built environment). What is more, on a micro level, I have become more aware of how close the abyss metaphor has been to the creative activities in which I continue to participate (as an urban explorer and sound artist, as well as how I conduct myself professionally in the classroom environment). My writings, my field recordings, my urban perambulations, my experimental music improvisations; it is possible to think of these dispositional manifestations as stories of the abyss. They are all creative and transgressive negotiations with human autonomy, and they all have an educational aspect (they all sit under the category of scholarship because they are all arenas of investigation shared with other people). My performances, my teaching, my efforts to have creative and critical writing published: in each instance I am throwing myself into the abyss in some way and making each act available for others to see or hear or read and take from it what they wish to take. With each act, I am risking negative feedback and rejection and dabbling in ego death (an occupational hazard/benefit that many people will recognize), all the while demonstrating a basic human right to freely determine my economic, social, and cultural development (Australian Human Rights Commission; Part 1, Article 1.1). I am simply doing what I believe I need to do to participate in, and contribute to, cultural conversations. For me, this is a sustainable means by which to live a meaningful and authentic life, recognizing that with each act I am expressing my human freedom. This is my disposition; this is my invariant principle.

A number of creative output options are available to me as I further focus my practice in keeping with my invariant principle. It seems appropriate to outline a selection of those that were given serious consideration even though they were eventually abandoned. I admit that, to some extent, this period of problem seeking and solving was impacted upon by the self-placed pressure that comes from a heavy investment in a creative process to make something that does justice to the effort expended, that justifies it. It is in a veritable *loop of justification* that I found myself struggling to move forward into new work, hence the time spent wandering into dead-ends; it took a few weeks before I arrived at an artistic project, a veritable mystory *Gesamtkunstwerk* that spoke clearly to the themes outlined under the banner of my invariant principle and that, most importantly, felt right to me as something that would not affect a kind of Sartrean bad faith. As Sartre wrote: "Consciousness is a being, the nature of which is to be conscious of the nothingness of its being" (86). People living in bad faith (*mauvaise foi*) are more like objects than conscious human beings, living as a *being-in-itself* instead of a *being-for-itself.*

Consequently, I have chosen to lay this process of filtration bare because it has played an important role in how the outcome decision is understood (we learn something of our object by stating what it's not); alternatively, this can be described as an act of pointing at things and then pushing them away from me (acts of identification and negation), to create a kind of psychological, communicable space (a clearing and void) in which a *remainder* can more clearly be seen.

I considered retaining writing as the creative nucleus, specifically writing about the abyss. Given that civilization started in Ancient Mesopotamia and with the invention of writing (Mesopotamian mythology marks the first time in history that people could write of the abyss), there is an opportunity to address this longitudinal narrative at its furthermost extremity (i.e., the technological driven present and its pervasive preoccupation with the internet, which I have already described a virtual void in which creative activity can now take place). As our newest platform for creative activity, I wondered whether *Tilt Brush* would bring the mystory to a satisfactory, if temporal, conclusion. Bringing this kind of abyss into the contemporary moment, I toyed with the idea of writing an essay on the esthetics of the abyss, using the *Tilt Brush* environment, so that myself and others could walk around the words, for example, making the reading process literally immersive. The memory of lights dancing on the harbor horizon, abstracting this notion of the virtual perambulation of lights through dark space, resonates well with the luminescent brush and handwriting/line work, of creatively placed punctuation, concrete poetry, etc. Yet, not having the financial support to realize such a project meant that it was not sustainable and, thus, living in a culture where sustainability holds significant ethical value, for me, the unsustainable practice was an unfavorable practice.

I went back to the drawing board and to thinking about the purpose and meaningfulness of this project. The mystory presents an opportunity to build a renewed sense of artistic purpose; this is what Ulmer invites us to embrace and appreciate. He does not ask that we change who we are or that we produce a particular kind of art over another kind, for example. Through the mystory, Ulmer invites us to think more clearly about what we already have at hand (warding off grandiose gestures, the heirarchicalization of creative modalities) but that, through a species of domestic blindness that advances over time (like a cataractic clouding of the ocular lens), might become less obvious to us and renders us more susceptible to disorientation and to the directions/directives of others.

Through the lens of the mystory, Ulmer assists us in using that extant resource—our own desire to engage creatively in the world—to the best of our abilities. Implicit throughout this assistance is Ulmer's commitment to creative cultures, which would mean very little if artists didn't share their work. Committing to a mystoriographical project demonstrates a sharing of this attitude—a sharing of the ontological position that creativity is a context of empowerment. Thus, from my perspective, Ulmer's mystory does not enable dependency; he doesn't make our fires for us or give us the fuel to burn. Rather, Ulmer's mystoriographical method seems to be much more closely aligned with creative resiliency building, helping individuals locate and take hold of their dispositional compasses so that they are prepared enough for whatever navigational and wayfaring challenges are ahead. Developing a mystory is a performance in its own right; it is a performance act, grounded in language and, by extension, a performative utterance—a *promise* to stay true to one's personal, metaphysical trajectory.

I was listening to an interview segment just a few moments ago, a part of which I would like to share with you in transcription. It is an interview with occult practitioner Bill Heidrick (Cybervue) in which he explains Aleister Crowley's *Oath of the Abyss*:

> As a formal oath in the context from which it arose, that is to say the Order of the Golden Dawn, for an exempt adept, a person at a mystical stage about to make a great journey across what is called the abyss, and the abyss is the division between the mundane and the spiritual, not more than that but that's simple enough to think, in our lives we have things that make sense and things that we sense. There's a lot of material stuff around there, and our lives are ordered by it. In our minds and in our souls we dream of a perfect life where everything is right and God is in his heaven or hers or its. Between these two there is a gulf. It is a purpose of the Exempt Adept, in life, to transcend this gulf and become what the Order of the Golden Dawn and A.·.A.·. [Astrum Argenteum] call a Magister Templi. The moment in which this voyage begins is a taking of the *Oath of the Abyss*. . . . At that moment it simply means you don't interpret anything. Everything is a communication of the divine with

> your soul. Don't try to make it say something it doesn't. Don't put a spin on it. Don't say "this looks like," or "I hear my angel speaking." Eliminate all that. There's no middle man, no messiah, no spokesperson, not even the shadow of a memory of what you learned as a child between you and the divine. That's what the Oath means. And only a person who's ready for that experience can actually take that Oath, otherwise they're wandering around jibbering at trees because they saw a shadow.

Aleister Crowley's *Oath of the Abyss*, in full, is as follows:

> 1. I, ___________, a member of the Body of God, hereby bind myself on behalf of the Whole Universe, even as we are now physically bound unto the cross of suffering: 2. that I will lead a pure life, as a devoted servant of the Order: 3. that I will understand all things: 4. that I will love all things: 5. that I will perform all things and endure all things: 6. that I will continue in the Knowledge and Conversation of my Holy Guardian Angel: 7. that I will work without attachment: 8. that I will work in truth: 9. that I will rely only upon myself: 10. that I will interpret every phenomenon as a particular dealing of God with my soul. And if I fail herein, may my pyramid be profaned, and the Eye closed to me.

I've known about the *Oath of the Abyss* since I was a teenager reading books by Anton LaVey and stumbling in a rather haphazard manner upon ideas and terminologies associated with will-based belief systems. Yet, now, despite brief internet-based attempts made in the distant past, is the first time that I have ever seen it written or had the opportunity to listen to someone offering a verbal explanation.

Despite this long-term disconnection, there is much about this Oath that seems familiar (i.e., notions of stepping into the unknown, of self-growth, of transgression into sites unseen, of personal freedom, of perambulation, of the abyss of being as a context for creativity and risk and authenticity). Crowley's writings are the basis for the various promulgations of Thelemic thoughts and practices that seem to me to be, each in their own way, humanitarian attempts to actualize an authentic life-politics. Who am I at my core? How do I work towards this authenticity in an ethical and sustainable way? These are the questions central to Thelema, but they are also central to the mystory. In view of this synchronicity, and drawing from my own long-standing interest in notions of the abyss, for a time I seriously considered developing work based on Crowley's *Oath of the Abyss*, not work that directly reiterates the tenets of the Order of the Golden Dawn of the A.·.A.·., like some kind of rookie proof of concept, but work that speaks to my own metaphysics and, thus, to my own invariant principle. I wanted to create my own circle, of sorts, if we may broaden our definition of circularity to include the unwavering reiteration of one's creative disposition, of the returning to the studio space as a form of self-articulating ritual. In witchcraft and occultism, the magical circle is cut into its cardinal points, known as *calling the corners*. These are the points marked out on the wind rose of a compass, perhaps the metaphorical compass to which Ulmer refers when explaining the mystoriographical imperative. Ulmer asks us to find our own orbit. So did Crowley.

> It sounds like such a simple thing. Planets have their orbit. Stars have their paths in the universe. Everything seems have a function. . . . So, Crowley's thing was "find your own orbit. Find what that orbit is. Find what your will is. Find what you're here to do, and then set to work to do it." He just happened to be quite an expert and quite an adept in exercising that will through the magical art of Western Hermeticism and classic Western ceremonial magic. But that doesn't mean that magic is the only path to this. Magic is only just one path for those who resonate to that kind of magical art form. I'm of the opinion that the greatest magicians in the world don't even know or care or need to know that they're magicians. They just found out what their will is in life and are setting out to do it. (Lon Milo Duquette, in Leak Project)

The reference Duquette makes to the idea of a personal orbit is recognizable; while I am not assigning Thelemic causality to Gregory Ulmer's mystoriograhical research method; nevertheless, we can appreciate that the mystory is also the expression of a will-based value system (built on a social-constructivist ontology of the *essence* of the authentic self). The mystory can also be understood as a will-based research method, "deposited" into "the consensual world where creative products must ultimately be made," as Briggs put it (194). If we are to work towards uncovering an invariant principle, are we not also seeking to elucidate and further articulate the nucleus of one's creative will, that is, the basis of their creative drive?

> Do what thou wilt shall be the whole of the Law. Love is the Law. Love under will. . . . This means that each of us stars is to move on our true orbit, as marked out by the nature of our position, the law of our growth, the impulse of our past experiences. (Crowley 9)

We don't need to follow Aleister Crowley's idiosyncratic brand of metaphysical thinking to recognize, quite readily, the esthetic and methodological correlation evident between the mystory and Thelema: both share a focus on the creative practicing of authentic, cultural, self-identity; what Ulmer calls invariant principle, Crowley calls *true orbit.* What Crowley calls the *nature of our position* and *the law of our growth*, lands remarkably close to Ulmer's take on the *dispositif* and on the *image of wide scope.* Thus, for a period of time, it made sense for me to draw insight from something like Crowley's *Oath of the Abyss*, exploiting the correlation as a means by which to approach to the project at hand by parallax. Both mark as an affirmation of human agency. Both seek to unravel the mystory of personal metaphysics through the identification and deposition of an idiosyncratic symbolism. In both instances an invitation is given, to commit to a leap into the unknown, to put one's self-cognizance at risk, to leap into the void of creative possibility and stick with it until the end, until such a time as one emerges from all of the tumbling about, from the pleasure and terror of the esthetic weave, to stand revised, and to observe what practical form has been taken.

As previously noted, Ulmer's notion of the mystory builds directly on the pioneering work in creativity research conducted by Gerald Holton and Howard Gruber. In addition, it is interesting that Gruber and Holton's key case studies share occult connections. W. B. Yeats's interest in the occult, spiritualism, mysticism, and astrology is no secret stemming back to his college days and remaining with him throughout his life. Yeats joined the *Hermetic Order of the Golden Dawn* in London sometime in March, 1890, remaining in association with the group for three decades, often making it the subject of his writing. During this time, Yeats's active interest in occult and esoteric practice was quite apparent in his works, such as the book *Ideas of Good and Evil* (1903) and an essay therein called *Magic* from 1901, which begins: "I believe in the practice and philosophy of what we have agreed to call magic, and what I must call the evocation of spirits, though I do not know what they are, in the power of creating magic illusions, in the visions of truth in the depths of the minds when the eyes are closed" (Yeats 23). Yeats would have kept the same company as Crowley, who became a member of the *Golden Dawn* in 1898.

It would be careless of me to make tenuous links between all Holton and Gruber's case studies and the occult as it is broadly understood. The fact that Wolfgang Amadeus Mozart was a member of the Freemasons meant that he would likely have gained a basic awareness of occult history and symbolism, and Jacques Chailley's book *The Magic Flute Unveiled: Esoteric Symbolism in Mozart's Masonic Opera : An Interpretation of the Libretto and the Music* (1992) is but a drop in the ocean of such qualitative investigation linking the great composer to the occult. It may be no more than a sign of the times that we find esoteric themata in the diaries of Virginia Woolf, in which she expresses disdain for the occult, as historian of English Literature Leigh Wilson points out:

> Nevertheless, Woolf's attempts to articulate what happens during artistic creation hover around the transformations of magic. Lily Briscoe, at the end of *To the Lighthouse* [my italics] (1927), is famously "haunted" by Mrs Ramsey, and, as the lighthouse is reached and Lily completes her painting, both are celebrated and perhaps produced by Mr Carmichael's ritualistic behaviour—he stands by her, looking like "an old pagan God"—and by the telepathic communion between them. (12)

Whatever connections can be discerned between the occult nuances of the work on which Ulmer builds his own, in the contemporary moment, I find the mystory's Thelema-like sentiment quite intriguing. Through this, I am reminded of how creative practice, as a will-based exercise concerned with the exposition and reiteration of personal symbolism, lends itself to rituals of self-affirmation.

I shall weave back to this thought in a moment, for now detouring into detail about how, before relocating from Western Australia to Melbourne, my wife Julie and I would visit this city once a year for a week or two. During this time, we would enjoy not knowing anybody who lived here, free to spend our time wandering around the streets, taking each day as a new and unscripted adventure. We rarely went to designated tourist locations. In some ways, I think that that preoccupation I had with long walks (when we finally made the move over) was in no small part an attempt to retain a tight grasp on the feeling of free play that Melbourne originally offered us and that I suspected, as we gradually settled into real lives as Melbourne residents, would eventually slip away.

During one of those annual excursions, which typically included our weaving in and out of second-hand book shops in the northern suburbs, I visited an independent bookshop that, between the philosophy and the cultural theory sections had a small area of shelving dedicated to occult publications. I remember fossicking through what was there and discovering that, among some well-worn editions of Crowley's writings, was a little paper pamphlet of perhaps little more than twenty-seven A5-sized off-white pages. It was called *How To Make Your Own Circle* and was, so far as I can now remember (it's strange that I can remember the title so much clearer than its contents), an instruction manual on the production of personal symbols for ritual practice.

I have always regretted putting this esoteric little pamphlet back on the shelf and leaving the shop (regret for not having embraced my intellectual curiosity). Perhaps if I had done so, it would by now have entered the higher ranks of irony as little more than a neglected holiday souvenir, buried indefinitely beneath old newspaper clippings and photographs with crimped edges in one of the air-tight plastic storage tubs that reach almost to the ceiling in the furthermost realm of our backyard shed.

It seems pertinent to share detail as to some of the work I considered developing. The idea was to produce music for float tanks, still with the concept of the abyss in mind, but also drawing from my experience in the creation of ambient sound recordings and experimental music. It wasn't until recently, thanks to the three-session gift voucher to Gravity Floatation Centre in Northcote, given to me by my wife and daughter as a birthday present, that I first got to experience what it was like to float in a sensory deprivation pod, with nothing to hear but my tinnitus and the intermittent sub-bass rumblings of trucks and trams passing in the distance. Lying in total darkness, slippery as a seal from the Epsom salts, I second-guessed my commitment to floating naked in the dark on a Friday morning. Why (apart from having been given a voucher) was I actively interested in depriving myself of the sensory stimuli so freely available to me in the outside world—the very same kinds of sounds that I am known to seek out and record. By gaining some kind of artificial respite—the closest I ever expect to get to the experience of nothingness—in this act of distancing and self-isolation, what was I gaining? At the time of writing, this question remains unanswered; no doubt future scheduled visits will need to take place before anything can sufficiently germinate and move towards hypothetical resolution.

Much like the *Tilt Brush* idea, I decided not to pursue production of music for float tanks. This decision was made in light of conceived accessibility restraints. First of all, it is not inevitable that people will be able to afford access to the technology, and I felt uncomfortable with the implicit exclusivity that such a project would have. Secondly, when speaking with friends and family about my own visit, the most common reaction was a strong aversion to the idea of floating in the dark with nothing but one's own thoughts as company. I'm fairly confident that my terms of description were generic enough that I was not unwittingly baiting a negative response; in my narrative, I had mentioned how interesting and relaxing the floatation experience had been, using words like *amazing*, and *worth doing again*, and so forth. At no point had I described the experience as disagreeable; as far as I was concerned, there was nothing disagreeable about it. The most common sentiment expressed by friends and family was a concern (which, I understand, might be put down to a kind of casual, social melodrama) that they would go mad, that they would freak out. I found this quite surprising; if I hadn't very recently gained first-hand experience of the floatation pod, I might have deemed myself too drawn in by the slick, new age marketing around floatation that directly references relaxation, recovery and sleep, creativity and learning, and pain relief. Whatever the perceived possible benefits, I felt like my audience would be too limited, and, besides, I realized from my own experience that floatation is, if nothing else, a personal experience; I struggled to imagine what value my sound art might add (i.e., what social function it might serve in this incredibly specific context), so I abandoned it.

Approaching this from a different angle (i.e., lying awake in the very early hours of the morning, staring somewhere vaguely towards the ceiling), if what we have is an opportunity to produce an affirmation of self and life, like Bush's mimetic dancing in the dark, or an *Oath of the Abyss*, or any gesture meant to encourage reflection on the human condition, what greater float tank is there to evoke than that in which we live in this universe? What greater material instance is there, of a body moving about in a seemingly infinite void, than that of the planet Earth itself, hurtling through space at 460 meters per second (this, the indiscernible velocity that we maintain even in a seated position), ever turning in an elliptical fashion around a sun with a circumference of approximately 93 million miles (150 million kilometers)—a sun that we feel on our bodies but that we shouldn't look directly at; viewing the sun only at parallax is highly recommended. The Earth is our ultimate float tank and each day, maybe, may require of us an *Oath of the Abyss* or some corollary manifestation—a commitment to life and to all that it has to give and take from us, and a commitment to everything that we have to learn from this experience regardless of our belief system (will-based or otherwise).

What is the music of the abyss? For me, a long time ago, it was epitomized by the UK version of the video clip for Kate Bush's "Wuthering Heights." The song's tele-visual broadcast shall forever remain in memory in the context of a lounge room within which, also, a three-year-old boy is dancing, a length of toilet paper flapping about quasi-calisthenically in the air. But now, nearly forty years later, I am lying on my back on the wooden deck, staring up into the star-filled and pristine night sky above Heathcote; lying here and enjoying a glimpse into the abyss in which we move at earth's orbital speed (like the stars of which Crowley speaks metaphorically), listening to the soundscape, the trees and the birds and the absence of cars or any other form of motor traffic to which I am accustomed to hearing, it would seem at times, without end in a city 110 kilometers away (68 miles).

As an adult, and father of a five-year-old girl, I have lost count of how many hours we have spent dancing together in our own lounge room and/or kitchen, where even the chugs and groans of the coffee machine have provided rhythm enough for a toe-tap or a bum-wiggle. Music is everywhere, at least it has always been an important part of our home-life. When my daughter was a toddler, I took her to a kids' weekly music class. Though she tired of the classes quite quickly, the CD of songs that she had been given, as part of her enrolment, was often being played at home, that is until I introduced her to the album *NO* by the American alternative rock band They Might Be Giants, at which point that became by far the favorite source of tunes to dance to. We listened to *Aphex Twin* when playing with Legos, referring to it as our building music; its glitchy, electronic perambulations seem to lend themselves to an activity that entails construction and destruction and strange geometric configurations that kind of look like something but only if you squint or tilt your head to one side.

How might we make artistic sense of this in the present? I sit and think about how Ulmer seems uninterested in privileging a particular kind of art; not in the business of telling us who we should be in the world. Rather, implicit in the mystory is an overarching reminder of how important it is to be conscientiously creative, to act with imagination and purpose, to make art meaningfully. Part of this entails listening to, and learning from, other peoples creative insights; I shall be attending Lawrence English's upcoming *Radical Listening Workshop* at the Substation in Newport. I'm curious about how it will all pan out, what this notion of radical listening is supposed to mean. I think I'm just as interested to see who else goes to these things, having not been much of a workshop-goer. As an act of learning, I typically prefer to do what I am doing at this very moment, which is to listen to the work of various artists, presently Australian sound artist Thembi Soddell, who I have recently learned about through another local artist—Eamon Sprod (Tarab). Sprod's continuing exploration, gathering, and recontextualization of sounds found in urban settings has resulted in several oblique sonic narratives of everyday detritus, decomposition, and clutter. He is also a wealth of knowledge when it comes to the creative processes of other sound-based artists, including Soddell. Listening to the *Topic* pieces that Soddell produced in partnership with Anthea Caddy, I am reminded of the psychological power of sound, its ability to embrace us with its dynamism; at times, in *Dissembling* for example, it's as if you can hear the emptiness and the darkness, and then the strings of a cello emerge, they churn and scrape, grind and contort. The cinematic drama builds to a climax and then nothing; we are back to listening to stirrings in the distance, waiting for the next tumultuous cycle, practicing patience, albeit ever tense in anticipation. Soddell and Caddy take the listener on a journey through the lightless spaces of the mind, along which he or she will hear and feel the miniscule becoming histrionic. When it is not illustrated by visuals, sound is free to provoke mental imagery; in "A Shut in Place," a forest breaks.

Work such as this is another welcome reminder of the power of sound to move the attentive listener; this kind of power doesn't just come along and present itself at the entrance to one's studio. I imagine that it requires a hunters' efforts and a surgical approach, built upon a kind of perambulatory mindfulness practice that takes the listener away from the computer and from the kind of sedentary work that impacts negatively on health and shortens life expectancy (WorkCover Queensland), and into the *epic* moments of the audible world. By *epic* I do not simply mean that which is conventionally large or grand—in scale or prestige—but rather that which has significance through its meaningfulness. "Speaking only of the *Kollosos*, [Jean-Pierre] Vernant declares: 'Originally, the word has no implication of size [taille]. . . . it will come to have this implication later, adds Vernant, only *by accident*" (Derrida 120).

In moments when I have realized I am lost, the world suddenly feels far more capacious; the streets become longer, the buildings and the trees seem to reach deeper into the sky than they did before. Epinephrine surges within the lost body, somehow changing the appearances of the world wrapped around it, just like it did when I was three years old and became separated from my parents at a public park. A kind stranger must have noticed my panic and walked with me until finally we found them; my parents were standing on the other side of a hedgerow, less than five meters away.

This notion of a perambulatory practice leads me to think of Auguste Rodin's sculpture *The Thinker*—highly prized by adherents to the Western European tradition of art, for sure, having become "one of the most celebrated sculptures ever known. Numerous casts exist worldwide, including the one now in the gardens of the Musée Rodin, a gift to the City of Paris installed outside the Panthéon in 1906, and another in the gardens of Rodin's house in Meudon, on the tomb of the sculptor and his wife" (Musée Rodin). Today I read a fascinating article, published by the National Gallery of Victoria (NGV), about the cast of *The Thinker* held in their collection. François Blanchetière and David Thurrowgood explain how Rodin specialist Professor Albert E. Elson, following his visit to the NGV in 1984, realized that the undocumented, Florentine-capped figure was, in fact, "the very first cast of *The Thinker*, executed in 1884 for the Anglo-Greek collector Constantine Alexander Ionides" and, thus, predating the better known version by about ten years. The authors describe the complex and highly sensitive conservation process that would result in the lost-wax cast's original patina, "obscured for longer than living memory," being once again revealed, along with "thousands of tiny white paint spots," most likely to have fallen out of the upper wall of the domed white library owned by Ionides—where the cast had once been kept (1).

However much we can admire the work's technical execution, in all honestly, I quite dislike the message it sends about thoughtfulness as a sedentary undertaking. Yes, the Dante figure is seated like an "athlete, meditating 'like a man of action at rest' . . . thinking in preparation for action. . . . a worker, a man of the people about to rise and act" (Blanchetière and Thurrowgood 4). Yet, while the mythological line of the sculpture is that it has "seemingly transcended its material form to become an idea permeating popular culture," in reality, I have difficultly giving credit to the notion of imminent action when the object of our attention is a bronze statue (Blanchetière and Thurrowgood 5). In this instance, the form of the work of art is condemned to betray its qualitative content; the two are incongruous. It's the kind of incongruity between sculptural material and subject matter that we can also detect in *Monument à l'Automobiliste* (1907); this marble sculpture, located in the Square Alexandre et René Parodi, Paris, was the first public sculpture to celebrate the automobile, referencing the world's first road race (Paris–Bordeaux–Paris) and its champion Émile Levassor. As Robert Hughes says:

> a stone car; the idea seems Surrealist to a modern eye . . . stone is immobile, mineral , brittle, cold. Cars are fast, metallic, elastic, warm. A human body is warm too, but we don't think of statues as stone men because we are used to the conventions of representing flesh with stone; there were no such conventions for depicting machinery. It was too new. (qtd. in Richardson)

To be honest, I'm not sure that this incongruity really matters (in much the same way that the incongruity of a stone car doesn't really matter, other than to demonstrate the limits of a representational convention in the face of new technological circumstances). But time has moved on, as has our thinking, and so the meaningfulness of works of art produced within the cultural contexts of the past, like the works being made every day, is always open to revision; unlike *The Thinker*, cultural meanings are not set in stone.

In any case, I really like the sculpture, and reading the NGV article has only made me want to see it in the flesh as it were, next time I am in the gallery's vicinity. But, for me, any meaningful reference to rising and action should be led by the example of someone rising and acting. For me, there is value in walking the talk, which this sculpture never could do, however much we might agree in the "universal sense" that the artwork is said to have taken on — that of the poet in the etymological sense of 'creator' (Blanchetière and Thurrowgood 4).

I feel most drawn to the model of the creator and the thinker who walks, an affinity affirmed during my visit to the Monash University Museum of Art's exhibition *Art as a Verb* (2014), a major survey of international practices that foreground process. Since that time, I have become increasingly interested in artists for whom acts of walking are vital to their practice (Bruce Nauman, Janet Cardiff and George Bures Miller; Simon Pope; Sophie Calle; Tim Knowles; and so many others interested in the intersections of walking and notions of identity, agency, psychogeography, and conservation, for example). Walking stimulates mental activity and a sense of personal well-being, plus it promotes physical health. If we take this as a benchmark then, on the contrary, sitting still like a statue across the decades, with one's head dropped down on one's fist, seems to offer no more than an image of the death of thinking. Sitting on a rock contemplating life is, for me, a total waste of time and it is regrettable that much of the work that many of us are required to do entails long periods of sitting in front of a computer; a whole day can go by and I don't even know what the weather is like outside (unless we choose to look it up on the internet or are fortunate enough to have a desk space located near a window). In any case, Rodin's masterpiece might be more appropriately called *The Shortening of Life and of the Hip-Flexor Muscle*, for example.

It is worth keeping in mind how grateful I am that I can walk, that long ago I was a three-year-old mobile enough to dance freely in a safe lounge-room environment, emulating a coordinated and agile woman dancing freely in a void inside the television. I'm grateful that I can go for a walk whenever I choose to and hear the sounds of roadworks and public transport vehicles spilling into my ears, taking a cue from R. Murray Schafer's comments on the imperialistic use of loud sounds (77), by taking the initiative to venture out and actively listening to *ditch diggers*, all aspects of which can easily be taken for granted (I started recording roadworks in 2012—a practice I would like to revisit at some stage, to pursue my interest in the power of mechanical sounds to compose abstract, sonic impressions of who we are as a creative and destructive society). Continuing on with this thought about mobility, I was interested by a conversation that took place between theorist Judith Butler and Sunaura Taylor. They are talking about disability, and at some point Sunaura says how she will use the expression *going for a walk* even though she is wheelchair bound (Taylor). This insight was interesting for the way it prompted critical reflection on possible tensions between the body and the built environment. Human mobility can be problematized in a variety of ways; one of the aims of the modernization of cities, Baron von Haussmann's nineteenth century renovation of Paris for example, has been to improve the circulation of fresh air and human traffic (civilian and military) by widening roads and installing pedestrian pathways. The assumption is that industrialization provides an infrastructure that is conducive to wandering, however one's gait might present itself. Yet, today, our public movements are often impacted upon by such factors as a lack of sidewalks or bike paths (in Melbourne, more work needs to be done to protect cyclists on dangerous roadways; Amsterdam is still a paragon of this endeavor). We could extend the frame to include movement restrictions experienced at international borders and consider how terrorism anxieties that are propagated by news media outlets have led to us giving up some freedom for the sake of safety.

There are also people who are able-bodied but somehow prevented from venturing into public spaces due to psychological conditions such as agoraphobia, a panic disorder affecting millions of people globally. There is an interesting case in Jacqui Kenny, the photographer who cannot leave her house due to agoraphobia, and so uses Google Street View to connect with people globally. Kenny (qtd. in Scott) says: "I really love the possibilities that comes with selecting and curating from billions of images that have been captured and frozen in time. The Google camera gives the images a really interesting point of view." Our culture might privilege visuality, but it is by no means the only way to connect, certainly not for the hundreds of thousands of people in Australia, for example, who are sight impaired. It could be beneficial to invest time in making binaural sound recordings of cafes, for example, so that people who would like to go to a café but can't, could at least still be able to listen to the shared cultural ambiences from which they otherwise remain excluded. This is a small idea on my part, for far greater interventions than this have helped foster positive life-experiences in others. Nevertheless, it's an idea that urges further thinking about the criteria with which I have been judging the value of my creative acts. There is value not only in sounds that move people but also in sounds that might capture movements on behalf of those for whom physical movement through physical space presents a challenge.

My decision is to go on treasure hunts for sound, sounds at home and sounds discoverable throughout the built environment, which might not be as exotic as making field recordings in the mountains of Taiwan, or of insects in Borneo, or as remote a location as the Galapagos Islands, Antarctica, Iceland, the Amazon, and the Arctic (though, I'm sure that would also be very nice), but what I do is no less meaningful. I don't feel like I need to get on a plane and travel for two days just to find something worth listening to, or to record something that would ultimately make me worth listening to when, upon my return, I began a new search for a captivated audience. The sounds I will be paying attention to will be those made by people and their machines, sounds made by the animals with which we co-exist, every day (autoethnographic). This means that I can walk through natural settings such as forests, or unnatural settings such as shopping malls. I can sit on a bench at a train or tram stop, or in a café, and know that sooner or later something will occur in the field that catches my attention (a trolley with squeaky wheels rattling past, a chorus of laughter). I can capture all this sonic information using my Roland CS-10EM Binaural Microphones/Earphones—designed to capture 360 degree recording of everything around their wearer, resulting in a far more surgical rendition of the sonic environment than stereo microphones, and still expect to find things that are sonically interesting. Binaural recordings, arguably more so than standard stereo recordings, are an excellent means by which to connect people with the past. A friend of mine once told me that, when he was a child, his father set up a binaural recording device in the family home, using a dummy head. As a result, today, this friend is able to listen to recordings of himself as a young person, okaying throughout the house. Because of the way binaural microphones capture sounds, affording a high level of accuracy when it comes to the placement of sounds in the sonic field, when listening back to one such recording, it's almost as if he was back in time, sitting on the floor of the lounge room of the past, listening to his younger self running circles around him.

I remember myself sitting on the brick wall at primary school, avoiding my invisible-rope anxiety, listening to the other kids chasing each other all over the playground, and feeling much further away from them than I physically was. I absolutely love the idea of a younger self unwittingly running circles around the older, listening self; invisible lines that traverse time and sonic space, like a spectre that haunts the present, given by technologically advanced devices and threatened with death by their eventual redundancy. This leads me to thinking once again about dancing to "Wuthering Heights"; if only I could hear, once again, what it sounded like to move around that room in that way (audio producers of all kinds will know that every room sounds different, which is why acoustic treatment is so highly recommended for studio-based recording situations). I know from photographs what the lounge room looked like, but what did it sound like? So much of that particular experience, of the body moved by the sounds that filled the room, is gone forever. There is such a disparity between the amount of time needed for that act to take place (once, twice, or several times) and the stretch of years that those early moments have rippled across since, almost imperceptibly.

The place of sound in relation to notions of haunting is a research focus that I'd like to pursue in greater length, and, already, I can see that there are a range of possible approaches available to me. One possibility would be to produce a site-specific binaural recording (of an art exhibition opening, or some such other public gathering) with the intention of playing this recording during a subsequent gathering/meeting in the same location: rooms that look nearly empty might sound full, as it is inhabited by ghosts, eliciting a sense of rupture or disconnection between what is seen (and what one expects to hear in keeping with that visual experience) and what is actually heard—ghosts, the real-time presence of which would become less discernible as the chosen room filled with people in actual time, while the recorded sounds of the past continue to play; they remain woven throughout the newly unfolding inter-personal soundscape, but they are hidden within it. They'd remain there but not there, we could say, sounds heard but unnoticed, as if to be drawing forth into existence some kind of latent trans-generational haunting (sound waves/lines mediating a dialogue with time—personal histories we cannot directly touch). Here, I have in mind Lisa Appignanesi's description of trans-generational haunting as "forgettings and rememberings [that] pace themselves through time" (qtd. in Clark).

The project presents an interplay of inside and outside, seen and unseen, drawing attention to notions of interiority, of invisible and psychological architecture; audio recordings of basements or other kinds of subterranean, infrastructural spaces (rethinking the role of urban exploration in my creative process), therefore, function metonymically as physical manifestations of deeper levels of consciousness. These are the physical and immaterial spaces in which we experience remembering and forgetting, and the emotional response we have to recalling things we wished we could forget (psychological haunting), or to the difficulty we might have preventing a pleasurable thought from fading away. There are myriad possibilities for exploring the disintegration of the boundaries between surface and depth (i.e., between what exists on a foundation and whatever is underneath that might emerge to trouble us). This could be interpreted as flaws in floors, through which memories might return, like puffs of dust that project upwards and outwards and disappear.

From Appignanesi's quote has come an idea to have the sounds of rooms organized by building and arranged for listening (on a gallery wall) as per a floor plan; each speaker could represent the positioning of the room from which the sounds it projects have been sourced. Another idea is to produce a room sound recording, play it inside another room and record that interaction, then play this newest recording inside a third room and record this interaction, and in this way produce a babushka doll effect. When applied to a single, multi-room building, this could speak to the notion of packing up a building (rather than packing up the objects situated inside the various rooms of a building). The previous approach could then be employed, whereby the sound portrait of one building is *unpacked* inside another building (much like when a business such as a private higher education provider relocates to a new address). Interesting acoustic ambiences might be discernible where the rooms of new and old buildings correspond and conflict, rooms haunting other rooms. It is important to note that rooms are meeting places, and that the French word for meeting is séance. Implicit, then, is that the investigative sound-based practice I pursue (not only because *practicing* requires perpetual return) is quasi-ritualistic; recorded sounds provide the context by which (through their creative manipulation) a veritable exhumation and negotiation of dead pasts takes place.

The broader term for what I am describing here is *sonic psychogeography*, denoting a range of opportunities to articulate identity and, thereby, to further understand the power of the built environment to impact on how we think, feel, and behave. The mood of the impact is variable, but it will in part be determined by how I treat the found sounds. As always, the possibilities I have sketched out remain open to revision. What will remain constant is my predilection for producing recordings or a variety of sonic phenomena and mining them for samples that, then, will become the raw material for soundscapes constructed either in the studio or in the context of a live improvisational performance. It will be important to not think too much about what the outcome of my recordings will ultimately be, not simply as a tactic for staving off pretension but as a means to keeping focus on the pleasure of listening.

It is not only the notion of dead sounds lingering that has importance, but also the life of audible realities and how we interface with them. Initially, I imagined how, by the very fact that I would be making decisions to record this and not that, selecting this sample and not that sample, my disposition would be discernible, present in whatever creative outcome the sounds ultimately fed. I had the idea that my capacity to demonstrate personal choice would be implicit in my acts and provide some oblique access to my ontology and epistemology, in line with the values that have been explored at length in this writing: freedom, perambulation, and so on. It was important for me to feel that I was working towards a creative outcome because it provided sharable evidence of these personal principles. Then, having organized my field recording equipment, I plugged in the Roland binaural headphones and went for a stroll through the shopping plaza located a short distance from where I live, my focus became less outcomes-based and more about exploring a sensory experience of a shared cultural environment, such as walking through a consumer center. The more I walked, first and foremost using it as an opportunity to become more acquainted with some updated gear, the more I found myself amid a mindfulness meditation — a conscientious perambulation. As the wind buffeted against my ears, I knew that this would result in audible interference on the recording and I was aware that it was something field-recordists often work to avoid. Perhaps, if I was working under contract to produce a blockbuster-film soundtrack, my attitude might have been different. But I wasn't trying to manufacture a marketable fiction; all I was trying to do was to venture out into my built environs and listen to its textures and rhythms — to experience a tiny part of the world in a new way, under renewed technological conditions. It was okay that moving air could be heard; it was okay if ever my bag could be heard rubbing rhythmically against my hip, perhaps accompanied by the sound of blown rubber soles tapping against hard surfaces.

As I walked, I became aware of how rarely I hear sounds straight-on and in a balanced way; by which I mean that, as I walked, hearing the world with slightly better clarity due to the fact that I had the gain turned up a touch on my headphones, I noticed the tram passing on my left; the three pedestrian crossing beepers playing in turn, clock-wise around the sonic field; the trolleys bashing against each other as a young male pushed past them on my right; and how, because I was moving through each exterior and interior space (which all have their own geometric and acoustic properties, and thus will each influence the way that sounds reverberate and travel in different ways), the balance of sound never sat perfectly like it might in a song or other carefully constructed audio composition.

This experience caused me to think again about parallax; through this mystoriographical process, I have come to understand parallax as a principle by which we negotiate the distanced past, and that this is a normal feature of our human condition. In rethinking about parallax, I realized that this word also appropriately describes our experience of the audible present, to which we have direct access. Sonic information is constantly moving around and past us; only under very strict and rare conditions do we have the opportunity to experience a completely balanced sound, whether in terms of its positioning on the sound-stage or in terms of the frequency bands being occupied. Parallax is not only relevant to a perceived deficit in memory; it is also relevant to how we might articulate a sensation of space, place, and identity in the contemporary moment.

In addition, although Guy Debord ("Theory of the Dérive" 62) articulated the *dérive* as "a technique of rapid passage through varied ambiences" ("Theory of the Dérive" 62), I would prefer to place less emphasis on haste, on rushing through the built environment, and more emphasis on mindful perambulation, on a kind of thoughtful loitering; for me, adopting a slow dérive as part of my investigative sonic practice would lessen the likelihood that "playful-constructive behavior and awareness of psychogeographical effects" ("Theory of the Dérive" 62) finds one brushing past a built environment's *at risk* inhabitants, for example the people living on the streets of the CBD in Melbourne, Australia, a city identified seven years in a row in the Economist Intelligence Unit's *Global Liveability Report* as the world's most livable city—people experiencing homelessness who sit in the margins of the pathways, quietly hoping to benefit from any spare change that pedestrians might give them (Chalkley-Rhoden). Much like those who sit without speaking, the lines I walk through the audio recordings I produce can also not be seen; at least they can be heard, swaying and weaving around other people and designed objects, in through one set of doors and out through another, above which an air-conditioner blows warm air down onto my head. Thus, we affect a conceptual shift beyond thinking about disposition to thinking about the changing positions of things (i.e., their displacement, which is exacerbated by the recording process because it is through the process of digital capture that I am able to transport sounds to other locations).

In terms of how the recordings will be treated, my primary interest is in continuing along the path that I have renewed over the past twelve months, which entails mining these longer recordings for fragments of various sizes (typically between one and twenty seconds in duration); collating them; then making selections to be layered and manipulated using digital processing tools (Ableton 9 Live, Push 2 controller for Ableton, a Korg kp3 and a Korg kp3+ used as dual stereo, outboard fx loops); and creating changes in pitch and speed, reverb and delay effects, loops and granular degradations, bit-crushing, scattering vocal fragments, with scope to include semi-coherent readings from the autobiographical writings of relatives (e.g., Dora Russell, who I am discovering through her own written words).

I took this approach during a performance I gave, at the time of this writing, last night; it was the first time I had the chance to play alongside Jen Tait, who I have known for a number of years and who I greatly respect as an artist. It is an almost inevitable consequence of a creative research method designed to exhume clarity around one's creative disposition that a lot of time will be spent articulating one's own personal practice. However, perhaps just as important as the impulse to make art and a willingness to share one's output with an audience, is the incredible creative reward that can come from collaborating with other members of an artistic community. My inaugural set with Jen, which was also the first time I had tested out my revised sound production rig in a live context, felt like a natural extension of the conversation we have had about our interests in improvised music, our thoughts on other genres, the memories we still have of our early childhood experiences living in England (this commonality being enhanced somewhat by the fact that we are the same age), and how the dispositioning of our lives through our unassociated migrations to Australia has stamped its mark on who we are. As so often seems to me to be the case when it comes to performing improvised music with other artists—when it comes to engaging in a temporal and spatial window of shared focus and attention, shared effort—it is a wonderful way to speak with each other and to invite others to listen in on that conversation. I am very grateful to be a part of a rich community of creative people who embrace each other's differences and, through them, are able to innovate sound-based perambulations together.

Thinking back to the performance, to the idea of participating in a creative conversation, it is worth commenting on the tone of conversation that might arise from my use of recordings of found sounds. For these, along with readings, recollections, etc, mean that all the sounds

I use will either implicitly or explicitly point to lapsed time; each sound piece that I produce exists in some kind of dialogue with time passed (the more personal the fragments, the more overtly mystoriographical this dialogue becomes). We can see, then, how mystoriography provides the apparatus; notions of haunting provide the experiential content; and sound remains the chosen, now consolidated, form of artistic communication. This is my way of developing, in audible and fragmentary dialogue with time, a gradually building and evolving, abstract sound portrait—an acousmatic record of events and experiences that is less a linear and completely coherent narrative (less literally diaristic) and more a conglomeration of fragments of inner-dialogue and semi-coherence, of self-talk and mutterings, of psychological feedback loops and repetitions; reflections on and of thoughts that cause troubled sleep and that, thus, need to be exercised, and exorcized.

Applicable to both improvisation and composition, this approach to sound production has the capacity to disorientate the listening experience by defamiliarizing fragments from the phenomenal world; it is just one of many possible means by which an artist may pursue a sound art practice beyond simply getting an audience together and playing back sounds that the artist likes. One example that comes to mind is the recent performance by Eamon Sprod that took place in a dirt-floored basement of a hairdresser's shop near where I live. The location was kept secret until moments before the performance was due to start, on a street corner, Eamon met those he had invited to attend and led us around the back of a building, through a metal gate, along a short walkway, and down into a trapdoor took us into the subterranean cavity. The space was dirty, smelled of mould, and cobwebs hung down from the floor boards above us like Halloween chandeliers. A dozen or so speakers had been positioned about the space, some of them behind boards that they would cause to vibrate. About six of us sat on little stools with the little colored buttons on midi-controllers and a laptop screen glowing in the darkness. Unfamiliar to the space, it was quite easy for me to close my eyes, forget where the walls were located, and get lost in the sounds of composition, imagining the room expanding and contracting in accordance with the acoustic and reverberant qualities of whatever was being heard, sounds from numerous other domestic and underground spaces imported into this one specific site, joined in the performance in ways that they would never otherwise have been (never under unmediated conditions). It was nice to feel as if the space in which we were sitting was breathing—a lung within the infrastructure, down into which we had climbed and from which we would eventually emerge. For me, it is a lovely poetic metonym of something that the late Stephen Hawking talked about, that just as the universe began with a big bang and a vortex from which our collective, cosmic past was expelled and that, although we move through time as the universe expands, eventually it will stop and everything will start to get sucked back in again as if all existence was contained within a single universal breath—a vital force several billion years in the making (119).

My attendance at Eamon's thought-provoking performance informs a train of thought that I have been following in recent weeks that, with all this emphasis on sound, for all my interest in the capacity of sound to defamiliarize and to disconcert a listener in a live setting, this possibility is hindered by the visible parameters of the performance environment (i.e., the walls, the ceiling, and the floor of the space in which a sound-work is shared, as well as the visible presence the other audience members). Or, at the very least, it should not be forgotten that visuality impacts on the meaningfulness of what is heard. Given my reference to haunting, it would be appropriate to disrupt visuality in some way. Within this generality, there is specificity that comes through thinking back to the UK version of the "Wuthering Heights" video clip, from remembering the historical writing I have produced relating to notions of the abyss, from reflecting upon my urban exploration adventures into the subterranean and infrastructural spaces of this built environment—expeditions during which total reliance on battery powered torches is almost always necessary. Specificity comes from recalling my recently abandoned idea to produce music for float tanks and my own first slippery encounter with sensory deprivation; through its scalability to something that is more readily sharable. Specificity comes through thinking about what it feels like to lie awake in bed at night staring at the ceiling, or on the wooden deck in Heathcote looking up into a pristine night sky and noticing all manner of thoughts moving about like shadows or ghosts in my mind's eye. A key visual factor in each example is the existence of near or total darkness. Each experience of darkness has fed into a broader meaning-making process and, therefore, has played a role in the formulation of my invariant principle. With all this in mind, performing music in the dark might seem like common sense; it is, at least, thoroughly consistent with the esthetics upon which my creative practice has been built (including some oblique cognizance of my unique professional circumstance as an experimental sound artist working in an industry-driven and ocular-centric design-arts school). These esthetics remain susceptible to infiltration by, and to influence from, the surrounding thickets of resonant memories.

For the first time in many years, I now remember how, when I was a teenager, listening to my favorite songs or talking with certain close friends always felt so much more interesting in the dark, more alive. Talking with the (bedroom) lights out was a practice frequently misunderstood by any parents in a household. But, it was mainly what we did to feel more closely connected (joined in the void, as it were, without actually touching) and therefore far more able to concentrate on our shared verbal communication. In the dark, a friend and I could be each other's most attentive listening partner, the privileged confidant, noticing every breath and whisper that it took to trace lines through each other's hopeful imaginings of what futures might lie ahead of us, of who we could become; sound was the context of materiality for these imaginings, bringing them into a sensory world in the form of linguistic utterances. What's more, in a lightless space no-one can see you, which means that it can also provide a person with temporary respite from any social difficulty or discomfort that they might experience when it comes to making eye contact.

Today, I am still very much drawn to that sense of an abyss of possibility and to thinking about how sound might be used to express it. In the context of this mystoriographical project, this pull of the abyss, this sense of a trailing and an induction into creative possibility, manifests as a decision to minimize visual distractions in the performance environment. I realize that turning out the lights in a performance space marks an unambiguous dislodgement of the privilege and authority afforded to visuality. More importantly, it is a sensory deprivation strategy that helps focus and intensify the listener's sonic encounter; it helps clear a space for the perambulatory imagination — make room for the inventive mind to wander. It is true that, on the side of practicality, working at odds with visuality resolves the sound artist's question of how to furnish their work with appropriate imagery or, to borrow Kara Walker's phraseology, to provide the onlooker with "adequate likenesses" (qtd. in Tatge and Shaffer). Closer to the point, by radically reducing the likelihood of visual distractions, darkness promotes personalized visualizations (in this sense it is similar in sentiment to Nietzsche's self-peering abyss, and similar in its ambitions to Brion Gysin's *Dream Machine*).

When speaking with friends and family about my visit to the sensory deprivation tank, I came to appreciate that some people find void spaces disquieting; for some, being in or near total darkness, let alone doing so while listening to warped samples and semi-coherent mutterings, could elicit a mood of psychological heaviness and anxiety. I imagine that part of this negative response is down to how difficult it becomes, in the dark, to identify and strategize around potential threats to personal safety. Of course, none of these friends or family meet *Vision Australia's* definition of an individual with legal blindness or low vision, of which there are 384,000 in this country (Vision Australia). An encounter with a darkened space might pose a challenge then, for sighted people are encouraged, by virtue of the kinds of digital media that pervade their everyday lives, to take vision for granted; darkness speaks back to the privileging of visual culture, curious as to the limits of its inclusivity and, in turn, the limits of democracy.

Adding to this, a study called "Crossmodal Induction of Thalamocortical Potentiation Leads to Enhanced Information Processing in the Auditory Cortex," published in the science journal *Neuron*, found that simulated blindness (for periods as short as one week) can improve our brain's ability to process auditory information (Petrus et al.,). Hey-Kyoung Lee, Associate Professor at John Hopkins University, reported that

> the loss of one sense—vision—can augment the processing of the remaining sense, in this case, hearing, by altering the brain circuit, which is not easily done in adults. . . . By temporarily preventing vision, we may be able to engage the adult brain to now change the circuit to better process sound, which can be helpful for recovering sound perception in patients with cochlear implants, for example. (qtd. in Gatlin)

Whether hearing improves or whether the loss of vision forces a person to pay much more attention to other sensory perceptions of the world, this study arms us with present-day confirmation of the neurological connectedness of seeing and hearing. As an artist working with processed field recordings, the applicable understanding that I come away with is this: by imagining new sonic encounters with the world and by bringing them to fruition as shareable artworks, including but certainly not limited to experimental soundscapes performed in the dark (at least, as dark as one can make a performance space without contravening occupational health and safety regulations) or in preparation for a private *listening-in-the-dark-through-headphones-is-recommended* scenario, this art can foster critical reflection on our habituated cultural environment; expose familiar things in defamiliarized ways; tamper with the shadows on the walls of Plato's cave, expose them as shadows to seek pleasure in their implicit negotiability, to consider how they haunt our truths, and then, when the lights go out, to wonder just what transformations will take place, like the shifts in the tonal values of the surfaces of harbor structures as the sun draws down towards the horizon line and, eventually, disappears.

5 Afterthought

If creative disposition is embedded in childhood experience, if the blue prints for all of a person's artistic activity to come, or, to put it in other words, if the invariant scaffolding is established near the beginning of life so that all one can do as life unfolds is find new pathways to its articulation, then what a creative person truly needs, for their practices to evolve, is what enables it to exist at all.

I began this project with the expectation that it would somehow lead me to a clarification of my creative nucleus, of a discernible artistic identity; for this and other reasons, it has been a worthwhile process. Although I have mentioned it in passing already, it is perhaps worth reiterating the point that this very project, the language with which it has been pursued, the privileging of written words (the grounding of creativity in literacy), albeit words that are often heard while they are written (for I have a tendency to speak while I'm writing), all point to a disposition of which I was sufficiently cognizant when I started. The purpose of the mystory has been to explore one's invariant principle. Not everyone will tackle this challenge, and whoever does will proceed in their own idiosyncratic way. It stands to reason, therefore, that this writing should be perfectly acceptable as a creative, mystoriographical outcome. But while this is sufficient in the short term, in the long term it is not enough; my impulse is to create work for the rest of my life, but I only intend to write this project once. Something else must follow what has, for me, been a wonderfully enjoyable seeding and irrigation and harvesting.

It might seem strange to think of the invariant principle, also, as something that is open to revision. But, if we can only approach it at parallax, then a step further around the orbit might lead us to conceive of it very differently than before; this is typical of a mindfulness activity wherein a person selects an object, such as a piece of fruit, an apple for example, something that they are used to handling in a habitual and automatic manner, and conscientiously making that process of nonjudgmental observation more prolonged, more difficult than ever before.

If we hold an apple in our hand and, instead of biting straight into it and jumping straight into a process of rapid mastication we hold it for a while, studying its colors and textures and experiencing it in a way that can seem alien to us (perhaps approaching it less like a fruit to be eaten and more like a sculptural artwork, reminiscent of the installation artwork Yoko Ono had on display the day she met John Lennon for the first time—the day he came into the gallery, grabbed it, and took a bite out of the side—to her dismay). Then, of course, the way we see, perceive, and conceive of it will have had the opportunity to change. This defamiliarization process can also be experienced when we repeat a single word over and over and over again until, eventually, we empty it of its meaning; through repetition, the word is dislodged from its denotation and becomes an abstracted sound event. You might wish to try it: apple, apple, apple, apple, apple . . .

Having started out with a view to the self in mind, is it surprising that I have arrived at a perspective that renders the self in a different way, albeit in miniature? In thinking of the earth as a float tank par excellence, I was led to another thought—a reimagining of what a creative imperative might be, a thought that does not focus on the most microscopic of divisions between us that might come about through nuanced personal experience but, instead, what joins us in all of our creative endeavors, that sustains our species.

The mystory has provided a theoretical framework on which I have tried to articulate the prime mover of my creative acts, the original chaos of all artistic activity that has taken place, and that will emerge throughout, my lifetime. In taking the social constructionist approach, the task has been to look outwards—to look to worldly experience and to mass-media exposure as a way of piecing together an impressionistic account of something that, thanks to the fallible human memory, can never be directly stated; we exist only in representation, like the shadows on the wall of Plato's cave. All the while, this outwards looking is done with one eye turned, reflexively, back onto the analyst in a constructively self-critical way. The ocular motif is significant; when the cave dweller is released, he steps out in to the world and, for the first time, is blinded by the bright light of the sun. As his eyes adjust, he gets to see all that exists—all that is visible in the daylight (as a playful paradigm test, I wonder how the meaningfulness of this famous allegory might have changed if the prisoner had stepped outside at night, but that's for another time). As it stands, it is as a result of seeing the world in a new way and by attempting to share this insight that the prisoner is himself viewed differently.

In this moment, when I think about what the nucleus around which all creative projects orbit, and to which they thus refer at parallax, I think it is the sun. If we are to go deeper than our cultural experience and look for what makes culture possible at all, perhaps what we really have to acknowledge is that giant sphere of molten plasma around which all the planets orbit, drawing invisible lines throughout the solar system.

> The sun's gravity keeps Earth in a stable orbit, preventing it from hurtling into outer space. It creates Earth's life sustaining weather and climate. Its light powers the photosynthesis that plants need to grow, which in turn produce the food and oxygen that animals need to eat and breathe. (National Geographic)

Driving the ritualistic practices of the British, Mayan, Incan, and Nordic sun cults of antiquity, for example, was reason; the sun rose into the sky everyday day, thus visible in a way no metaphysical being could ever be. We owe so much to the sun. This giant star, comprising 99.86% of the solar systems mass, has existed for approximately four and a half billion years and may well have as much life ahead of it. As far as prime movers are concerned, perhaps we can think of the sun as the invariant principle to which all our creative activities can be traced, that giant ball of fire to which they implicitly point, like a needle on a compass pointing North. All life depends on the sun and, when it dies (as all stars eventually do), the earth will cease to exist. Once consumed by the sun, all that's been created will be gone; all that haunts and all that is haunted, will cease.

Works Cited

Baird, Iain. "Colour Television in Britain." *The National Science and Media Museum*, 2011, blog.scienceandmediamuseum.org.uk/colour-television-britain/. Accessed 22 Jan. 2018.

Baker, Lynne Rudder. "What Is Human Freedom?" *Philosophical Workshop on Free Will*. San Raffaele University, 2005, people.umass.edu/lrb/files/bak-05whaM.pdf. Accessed 29 Nov. 2016.

Bakhtin, Mikhail. *Speech Genres and Other Late Essays*. 2nd ed. Translated by Vern W. McGee, edited by Caryl Emerson and Michael Holquist, Texas UP, 1986.

BBC & Arts Council England. "Bill Viola, The Dreamers." *YouTube*, uploaded by Blain Southern, 30 Aug. 2017, www.youtube.com/watch?v=tGNSyDl2NWo.

Bignell, Jonathan. *Media Semiotics: An Introduction*. Manchester UP, 2002.

Blanchetière, François, and David Thurrowgood. "Two Insights into Auguste Rodin's the Thinker." *Art Journal*, no. 52, 2013, www.ngv.vic.gov.au/essay/two-insights-into-auguste-rodins-the-thinker/. Accessed 21 Feb. 2018.

Braun, Virginia, and Victoria Clarke. "Using Thematic Analysis in Psychology." *Qualitative Research in Psychology*, vol. 3, no. 2, 2006, pp. 77–101.

Briggs, John. *Fire in the Crucible: Understanding the Process of Creative Genius*. Red Wheel and Weiser, 1990.

Brooker, Peter. *A Glossary of Cultural Theory*. 2nd ed., Hodder Arnold, 2003.

Camus, Albert. *The Myth of Sisyphus and Other Essays*. Translated by Justin O'Brien, Vintage Books, 1991.

Carles, Pierre, director. *La Sociologie Est Un Sport De Combat*. Pierre Bourdieu, Cara M. 2001.

Chailley, Jacques. *The Magic Flute Unveiled: Esoteric Symbolism in Mozart's Masonic Opera: An Interpretation of the Libretto and the Music*. Inner Traditions Bear and Company, 1992.

Chalkley-Rhoden, Stephanie. "World's Most Liveable City: Melbourne Takes Top Spot for Seventh Year Running." *ABC News*, 16 Aug. 2017, www.abc.net.au/news/2017–08–16/melbourne-named-worlds-most-liveable-city-for-seventh-year/8812196.

Chang, Charis. "War on Waste: Craig Reucassel Reveals the Shocking Truth About Our Bananas." *News.com.au*, 16 May 2017, www.news.com.au/finance/business/retail/war-on-waste-craig-reucassel-reveals-the-shocking-truth-about-our-bananas/news-story/ddd59b65712f4649fc74b3f803520776.

Clari, Michela. "Dispositif." *Collins French Dictionary*, edited by Lorna Knight, HarperCollins Publishers, 2006.

Clark, Alex. "Haunting across the Generations." *The Guardian*, 15 Apr. 2000, www.theguardian.com/books/2000/apr/15/fiction.reviews.

"Cliff." *The New Shorter Oxford English Dictionary*. 4th ed., 2 vols. 1993.

Connor, Steven. "Ears Have Walls: On Hearing Art." *Sound*, edited by Caleb Kelly, Whitechapel Gallery and MIT Press, 2011, pp. 129–39.

"Cote." *The New Shorter Oxford English Dictionary*. 4th ed., 2 vols. 1993.

Cowling, Rob, director. *Genius of the Modern World, Marx*. BBCFour, 2017.

"Creativity and the Pursuit of Excellence." *Academy of Ideas*. 21 Jan. 2014, http://academyofideas.com/2014/01/creativity-and-the-pursuit-of-excellence/.

Cristin, Renato. *Heidegger and Leibniz: Reason and the Path*. Translated by Gerald Parks, Kluwer Academic Publishers, 1998.

Crombie, Neil, director. *Status Anxiety*. Alain de Botton, BBC , 2004.

Crowley, Aleister. *The Book of the Law*. Weiser Books, 1976.

Debord, Guy. "Théorie De La Dérive." *Internationale Situationniste*, no. 2, 1958.

—. "Theory of the Dérive." *Situationist International Anthology*. Translated by Ken Knabb, edited by Kenn Knabb, Bureau of Public Secrets, 1981.

Dee, Jon, Pat Cash, and Tina Jackson. "Fast Facts on Food Waste." *Foodwise*. Government of South Australia, 2017, www.foodwise.com.au/foodwaste/food-waste-fast-facts/.

Derrida, Jacques. *The Truth in Painting*. Translated by Geoff Bennington and Ian McLeod, Chicago UP, 1987.

"Docile." *The New Shorter Oxford English Dictionary*. 4th ed., 2 vols. 1993.

Duquette, Lon Milo. "Oto, Master Occultist, Lon Milo Duquette Talks Enochian Magick, Hermetics, Thelema." *YouTube*, uploaded by Leak Project, 25 Jan, 2017, https://www.youtube.com/watch?v=3M0FOaAzqWI.

Durant, Will. *The Story of Philosophy: The Lives and Opinions of the World's Greatest Philosophers*. Pocket Books, 1991.

Elkann, Alain. "Tracey Emin." *Alain Elkann Interviews*. 28 Dec. 2014, alainelkanninterviews.com/tracey-emin/.

Emigh, John. *Masked Performance: The Play of Self and Other in Ritual and Theatre*. Pennsylvania UP, 1996.

Endres, William. *Rhetorical Invention in the Book of Kells: Image and Decoration on Their Flight to Meaning.* 2008. Arizona State University, PhD dissertation.

English, Lawrence. "We Can See Someone Looking, but Can We Hear Someone Listening?" *YouTube*, uploaded by TEDx Talks, 21 Dec. 2016, www.youtube.com/watch?v=FA9hkqFbx1k.

"Epistemology." *The New Shorter Oxford English Dictionary.* 4th ed., 2 vols. 1993.

Figueiredo, Sergio. "Theopraxis and the Future of H'mmm in the University: An Interview with Gregory L. Ulmer." *Journal for Cultural and Religious Theory*, vol. 16, no. 1, 2016, www.jcrt.org/archives/16.1/InterviewUlmer.pdf.

Foucault, Michel. "The Confession of the Flesh." *Power/Knowledge Selected Interviews and Other Writings*, edited by Colin Gordon, Vintage, 1980, pp. 194-228.

Franken, Robert E. *Human Motivation.* Brooks/Cole, 1993.

Freud, Sigmund. "The Uncanny." *The Standard Edition of the Complete Psychological Works of Sigmund Freud: An infantile neurosis and other works (1917—1919), Volume 17.* Translated by James Strachey and Anna Freud, Hogarth Press, 1995, pp. 217-56.

Garcia, Paul. "Walking in an Exaggerated Manner around the Perimeter of a Square." *Not Coming to a Theater Near You.* 1 Mar. 2006, notcoming.com/reviews/walkingsquare/.

Gasper, Phil. "Capitalism and Alienation." *International Socialist Review*, no. 74, 2010, isreview.org/issue/74/capitalism-and-alienation.

Gatlin, Latarsha. "Simulated Blindness Can Lead to Recovery of Lost Hearing, Researchers Say." *Hub*, Johns Hopkins University, 6 Feb. 2014, hub.jhu.edu/2014/02/05/blindness-hearing-loss/.

Geiger, John. *Chapel of Extreme Experience: A Short History of Stroboscopic Light and the Deam Machine.* Soft Skull Press, 2003.

Giddens, Anthony. *Modernity and Self-Identity: Self and Society in the Late Modern Age.* Stanford UP, 1991.

—. *Sociology.* Polity, 1998.

Gleitman, Henry, Alan J. Fridlund, and Daniel Reisberg. *Psychology.* 6th ed., Norton & Company, 2004.

Gorenberg, Rita. "New Study Shows Soap Washes Down the Drain, but Germs Don't." *The Clorox Company*, 2 Dec. 2014, http://www.multivu.com/players/English/7359251-clorox-and-nsf-study-shows-which-surfaces-have-most-germs-in-homes-with-kids/.

Gray, Richard. "Women Wearing Red Send Signals That Attract Men." *The Telegraph*, 26 Feb. 2012, www.telegraph.co.uk/news/science/science-news/9105879/Women-wearing-red-send-signals-that-attract-men.html.

Green, Clinton, and Carmen Chan. "Improv Idol." *Improv Idol*, 2015, https://improvidol.com/about/.

Grey, Pat, and Ed Grey. *Fungi Down Under: The Fungimap Guide to Australian Fungi*. Fungimap Inc., 2005.

Gruber, Howard. "Darwin's Tree of Nature and Other Images of Wide Scope." *On Aesthetics in Science*, edited by Judith Wechsler, Birkhäuser, 1988, pp. 121–42.

Gruber, Howard E., and Katja Bödeker, editors. *Creativity, Psychology and the History of Science*. Vol. 245. Springer, 2005.

Hawk, Byron. *A Counter-History of Composition: Toward Methodologies of Complexity*, edited by David Bartholomae and Jean Ferguson Carr, Pittsburgh UP, 2007.

Hawking, Stephen. *A Brief History of Time*. Bantam, 1998.

"Heath." *The New Shorter Oxford English Dictionary*. 4th ed., 2 vols. 1993.

"Heathen." *The New Shorter Oxford English Dictionary*. 4th ed., 2 vols. 1993.

Hebdige, Dick. *Subculture: The Meaning of Style*. Routledge, 2012.

Hegarty, John. *Hegarty on Creativity: There Are No Rules*. Thames & Hudson, 2014.

Hegarty, Paul. *Noise/Music: A History*. Continuum, 2008.

Heidegger, Martin. *Nietzsche Volumes One and Two*. HarperCollins, 1991.

Herbert, Martin. "Infinity's Borders: Ryoji Ikeda." *Sound*, edited by Caleb Kelly, Whitechapel Gallery and MIT Press, 2011, pp. 162–65.

"How to Be Positive—Buddhist Meditation." *YouTube*, uploaded by New Kadampa Tradition, 23 Jul. 2015, www.youtube.com/watch?v=goo2IMA-nBw.

"Ing." *The New Shorter Oxford English Dictionary*. 4th ed., 2 vols. 1993.

International Covenant on Economic, Social and Cultural Rights. Australian Human Rights Commission. 2012, www.humanrights.gov.au/international-covenant-economic-social-and-cultural-rights-human-rights-your-fingertips-human-rights.

"Jack Parsons & the Oath of the Abyss." *YouTube,* uploaded by Cybervue, 21 Jun. 2008, www.youtube.com/watch?v=wOyOcjA_T6k.

James, David. "How to Get Clear About Method, Methodology, Epistemology and Ontology, Once and for All." *YouTube*, uploaded by ESRC Wales Doctoral Training Centre, 9 Apr. 2015, www.youtube.com/watch?v=b83ZfBoQ_Kw.

Jeans, James W. *Litigation*. Kluwer Law Book Publishers, 1986.

Kadampa Melbourne. "Gen Kelsang Dornying on Meditation and Mindfulness." *YouTube*, 19 Jan. 2014, https://www.youtube.com/watch?v=hShadNWgIkk.

Kidel, Sam. "The Politics of Ambience." Oxford Brookes University, 1 Dec. 2016, www.thepoliticsofambience.co.uk/contact/.

Kirkpatrick, Betty. *The Concise Oxford Thesaurus*. Oxford UP, 1997.

Knight, Richard Payne, and Thomas Wright. *Sexual Symbolism: A History of Phallic Worship*. Dover Publications, 2006.

Kogi, Martin, editor. "Bill Viola Interview: Cameras Are Soul Keepers." *YouTube*, uploaded by Louisiana Museum of Modern Art, 18 Apr. 2013, www.youtube.com/watch?v=uenrts2YHdI&feature=youtu.be.

Lockwood, Louise, director. *Why Beauty Matters*. Roger Scruton, BBC Two, 2009.

Lubbock, Tom. "Great Works: Dynamism of a Dog on a Leash (1912) Giacomo Balla." *The* Independent, 4 Sep. 2009, www.independent.co.uk/arts-entertainment/art/great-works/great-works-dynamism-of-a-dog-on-a-leash-1912-giacomo-balla-1781174.html.

Macey, David. *Dictionary of Critical Theory*. Penguin Books, 2000.

Mackay, Hugh. "Softening Us up for Surveillance." *InPsych*, vol. 39, no. 4, 2017, pp. 22–23.

Maslow, Abraham. "A Theory of Human Motivation." *Psychological Review*, no. 50, 2000, pp. 370–96.

Master Class. "Frank Gehry Teaches Design & Architecture | Official Trailer." *YouTube*, 18 February 2017, www.youtube.com/watch?v=Az-m56vUjgw.

McLeod, Saul. "Erik Erikson." *Simply Psychology*. 2017, www.simplypsychology.org/Erik-Erikson.html.

McLuhan, Marshall. *Understanding Media: The Extensions of Man*. MIT Press, 1994.

Mendelsohn, Ashley. "The Unexpected Low-Tech Solutions That Made the Guggenheim Bilbao Possible." *ArchDaily*, 18 Oct. 2017, www.archdaily.com/881663/the-unexpected-low-tech-solutions-that-made-the-guggenheim-bilbao-possible.

Merck, Mandy. "Bedtime." *The Art of Tracey Emin*, edited by Mandy Merck and Chris Townsend, Thames and Hudson, 2002.

Mitchell, W. J. T. "There Are No Visual Media." *Sound*, edited by Caleb Kelly, Whitechapel Gallery and MIT Press, 2011, pp. 76–79.

"Momentum." *Merriam-Webster*. 2016, www.merriam-webster.com/dictionary/momentum.

"Morality." *The New Shorter Oxford English Dictionary*. 4th ed., 2 vols. 1993.

Morrissette, Bruce. Introduction. *Jealousy*, by Alain Robbe-Grillet, Grove Press, 1981, 1–10.

Murtaza, Niaz. "Pursuing Self-Interest or Self-Actualization? From Capitalism to a Steady-State, Wisdom Economy." *Ecological Economics*, no. 70, 2011, pp. 577–84.

National Geographic. "Sun 101." *YouTube*, 3 Dec. 2016, www.youtube.com/watch?v=2HoTK_Gqi2Q.

Nauman, Bruce, director. *Bruce Nauman: Setting a Good Corner (Allegory and Metaphor)*. National Galleries Scotland, 2015.

Nelson, Robert. *The Jealousy of Ideas: Research Methods in the Creative Arts*. Ellikon, 2009.

Nietzsche, Friedrich. "Thus Spoke Zarathustra: A Book for All and None." Translated by Walter Kaumann, *The Portable Nietzsche*, edited by Walter Kaumann, Penguin Books, 1982.

Nietzsche, Friedrich. *Beyond Good and Evil: Prelude to a Philosophy of the Future*. Translated by R. J. Hollingdale, Penguin Books, 1990.

Norden, Eric. "Marshall McLuhan Interview from Playboy, 1969." *The Marshall McLuhan Center on Global Communications*, edited by Phillip Rogaway, University of California, 2007, web.cs.ucdavis.edu/~rogaway/classes/188/spring07/mcluhan.pdf.

Northedge, Andy. "Three Decades of Open University Television Broadcasts: A Review." *History of the OU*. 2011, www.open.ac.uk/blogs/History-of-the-OU/?p=1897.

"Ontology." *The New Shorter Oxford English Dictionary*. 4th ed., 2 vols. 1993.

Perec, Georges. *Species of Space and Other Pieces*. Translated by John Sturrock, Penguin, 2008.

Perkins, Jenni. "Stable Home Life Key to a Child's Development." *The West Australian*, 5 May 2015, thewest.com.au/opinion/stable-home-life-key-to-a-childs-development-ng-ya-111542.

Petrus, Emily, et al., "Crossmodal Induction of Thalamocortical Potentiation Leads to Enhanced Information Processing in the Auditory Cortex." *Neuron*, vol. 81, no. 3, 2014, pp. 664–73.

Pigrum, Derek. "The 'Potential Space' of Transitional Creative Notation." *Text*, no. 13, 2012.

Plato. *The Last Days of Socrates*. Translated by Hugh Tredennick, Penguin Group, 1969.

Pollman, Judith, "Memory: Concepts and Theory." *Research Institute for History*. Leiden University, 12 Aug. 2014, www.hum.leiden.edu/history/talesoftherevolt/approach/approach-1.html.

Prescott-Steed, David. "Black Sea Abyss: Chaos and Writing in Ancient Mesopotamia." *TRANS—Revue de littérature générale et comparée*. no. 6, 2008, trans.univ-paris3.fr/IMG/pdf/c_Prescott_trans.pdf.

—. "Playing in the Abyss: Generating Potential Space." *LITERA: Batı Edebiyatları Dergisi*, vol. 2, no. 2, 2008, pp. 41–60.

—. "Dérive and Defamiliarisation: Seeking Alternative Solutions Amid Institutional Architecture." *Subjectivity, Creativity and the Institution*, edited by Christopher Crouch, Brown Walker Press, 2009.

—. "Nemo's Abyss: The Deferral of Undecidability." *Philament: An Online Journal of the Arts and Culture*, no. 16, 2010, pp. 34–49. www.philamentjournal.com/issue16/.

—. "Improvising Everyday Life: The Performance of Practice-Led Research." *Creative Industries Journal*, vol. 4, no. 1, 2011, pp. 71–85.

—. "A New Frontier for Visual Culture: Thoughts on the Production and Consumption of Digital Deep-Sea Imagery." *KINEMA: A Journal for Film and Audiovisual Media*, Fall 2012, pp. 77–90.

—. "Frostbite on My Feet: Representations of Walking in Black Metal Visual Culture." *Helvete: A Journal of Black Metal Theory*, no. 1, 2013, pp. 45–68.

—. "Intersections of Creative Praxis and Urban Exploration." *The Journal for Artistic Research*, no. 9, 2015, jar-online.net/index.php/issues/view/491.

—. "Practical Theory: A Creative Approach to Design-Arts Education in Melbourne, Australia." *Textshop Experiments*. no. 2, 2016. textshopexperiments.org/textshop02/practical-theory-a-creative-approach-to-designarts-education/.

"Procrastinate." *The New Shorter Oxford English Dictionary*. 4th ed., 2 vols. 1993.

Radios-TV. "Ultra Black & White Hybrid in 1977." *Radios-TV: The Home of Early Colour Television*. 16 Oct. 2016, www.radios-tv.co.uk/black-white-hybrid-in-1977/.

Ramsey, Michael, director. *The Cave: An Adaptation of Plato's Allegory in Clay*. 2007. Bullhead Entertainment LLC.

Richardson, David Lewis, director. *Shock of the New: Mechanical Paradise*. Robert Hughes, BBC, 1980.

Robsville, Sean. "The Emptiness of the Mind in Kadampa Buddhism." *Rational Buddhism: The Scientific and Philosophical Basis for Buddhist Belief and Practice*, 28 Feb. 2013, rational-buddhism.blogspot.com.au/2013/01/the-emptiness-of-mind-in-kadampa.html.

Royal Academy of Arts. "Tracey Emin Ra Talks About 'My Bed.'" *YouTube*, 1 Jul. 2014, www.youtube.com/watch?v=IylzsJk759M.

Sartre, Jean-Paul. *Being and Nothingness*. Translated by Hazel E. Barnes, Washington Square Press, 1956.

Schafer, R. Murray. *Soundscape: Our Sonic Environment and the Tuning of the World*. Destiny Books, 1994.

School of Life. "In Praise of Bias." *YouTube*, 23 Jan. 2018, www.youtube.com/watch?v=ZbPt66TYsFM.

Scott, Ellen. "Agoraphobic Woman Travels the World with Google Street View." *Metro*, 12 Jul. 2017, metro.co.uk/2017/07/12/woman-terrified-of-leaving-the-house-travels-the-world-with-google-street-view-6773513/.

Sebald, W. G. *Austerlitz*. Translated by Anthea Bell, Penguin Books, 2011.

—. *On the Natural History of Destruction*. Translated by Anthea Bell, Modern Library, 2004.

Sibley, Adrian, director. *The Kate Bush Story: Running Up That Hill*. Kate Bush, BBC, 2014.

Silver, Victoria, director. *Goldsmiths: But Is It Art?* BBC, 2010.

Solnit, Rebecca. *A Field Guide to Getting Lost*. Penguin Books, 2006.

Stallabrass, Julian. *High Art Lite: British Art in the 1990s*. Verso Books, 2001.

State Government Queensland, WorkCover Queensland. *Are You Going to Be Upstanding in 2017*? 1 March 2017, https://www.worksafe.qld.gov.au/forms-and-resources/newsletter/esafe-newsletters/esafe-editions/esafe/february-2017/are-you-going-to-beupstanding-in-2017.

Stuart, Mel, director. *Willy Wonka & the Chocolate Factory*. Performance by Gene Wilder, Paramount Pictures, 1971.

Stucky, Nathan, Cynthia Wimmer, and Richard Schechner, editors. *Teaching Performance Studies*. 1st ed., Southern Illinois UP, 2002.

Student Edge. "I Wanna Be an Architect—a Day in the Life of an Architect." *YouTube*, 11 Dec. 2017, www.youtube.com/watch?v=asdgRAjGK-M.

Taller de Escritura Fuentetaja. "Sebald Y La Fotografía." *YouTube*, 3 Apr. 2014, https://www.youtube.com/watch?v=PYoIbYgcADw.

Tatge, Catherine and Deborah Shaffer, directors. *Art21: art in the twenty-first century, season 2*. Kara Walker, PBS Home Video, 2003.

Taylor, Andrew. "Cuts of More Than $100 Million to the Arts Could Be 'Devastating.'" *The Sydney Morning Herald*, 14 May 2014, www.smh.com.au/entertainment/art-and-design/cuts-of-more-than-100-million-to-the-arts-could-be-devastating-20140514-zrbxh.html.

Taylor, Astra, director. *Examined Life*. 2009. Zeitgeist Films.

Taylor, Richard. *Ethics, Faith and Reason*. Prentice Hall, 1984.

"The Thinker." *Musée Rodin*, Paris, www.musee-rodin.fr/en/collections/sculptures/thinker. Accessed 21 Feb. 2018.

Throsby, David, and Anita Zednick. "Do You Really Expect to Get Paid? An Economic Study of Professional Artists in Australia." *Research and Strategic Analysis*. Australia Council for the Arts, 2010, www.australiacouncil.gov.au/workspace/uploads/files/research/do_you_really_expect_to_get_pa-54325a3748d81.pdf.

Trigwell, Keith, et al., "Scholarship of Teaching: A Model." *Higher Education Research & Development*. vol. 19, no. 2, 2000, www.researchgate.net/profile/Mike_Prosser/publication/242516917_Scholarship_of_Teaching_A_Model/links/540ea5dd0cf2d8daaacd55eb.pdf.

Tyrnauer, Matt. "Architecture in the Age of Gehry." *Vanity Fair*, 2010, www.vanityfair.com/culture/2010/08/architecture-survey-201008?currentPage=all.

Ulmer, Gregory. *Teletheory*. Atropos Press, 2004.

—. "The Chora Collaborations." *Rhizomes*. no. 18, 2008, www.rhizomes.net/issue18/ulmer/index.html.

Vardouli, Rodanthi. "Gregory L. Ulmer [Q&a] on Mystoriography." *YouTube*, 7 Mar. 2014, www.youtube.com/watch?v=eVrk1GYEfLE.

—. "Gregory L. Ulmer on Mystoriography (Teletheory, 1989)." *YouTube*, 7 Mar. 2014, https://www.youtube.com/watch?v=Sb742GVetsM.

Vision Australia. "Blindness and Vision Loss." 2 Mar. 2018, www.visionaustralia.org/information/newly-diagnosed/blindness-and-vision-loss.

Webb, Carolyn. "Kate Bush Music Video Mimed by Thousands for Most Wuthering Heights Day Ever." *The Age*, 29 November 2016, www.theage.com.au/victoria/guys-and-girls-in-red-dresses-line-up-to-mimic-kate-bush-20160211-gmryk7.html.

Wilson, Leigh. *Modernism and Magic: Experiments with Spiritualism, Theosophy and the Occult*. Edinburgh UP, 2012.

Winnicott, Donald W. *Playing and Reality*. Routledge, 1971.

—. "The Location of Cultural Experience." *Transitional Objects and Potential Spaces: Literary Uses of D. W. Winnicott*, edited by P. L. Rudnytsky, Columbia U, 1993, pp. 3–12.

Wittgenstein, Ludwig. *Tractatus Logico-Philosophicus*. Translated by David Pears and Brian McGuinness. Routledge, 2016.

Wollstonecraft, Mary. *A Vindication of the Rights of Woman*. 2nd ed., Dover Publications, 1996.

Yeats, William Butler. *The Collected Works in Verse and Prose of William Butler Yeats*. 2015, http://www.gutenberg.org/ebooks/49608.

Young Rojahn, Susan. "Memory Is Inherently Fallible, and That's a Good Thing." *MIT Technology Review*, 9 Oct. 2013, https://www.technologyreview.com/s/520156/memory-is-inherently-fallible-and-thats-a-good-thing/.

Zola, Émile. *The Ladies' Paradise*. Translated by Brian Nelson, Oxford UP, 1998.

Index

About the Author

David Prescott-Steed is an artist and writer whose creative practice is focussed on found sound processing and improvisation. His work has been presented at The Politics of Ambience (Oxford Brookes University, UK), PNEM New Music Festival (The Netherlands), Kinokophonography (London and NY), (h)ear XL II: Multimedia Sound Art Exhibition (The Netherlands), MATLIT: Materialities of Literature (Portugal) and the National Gallery of Victoria's Melbourne Now exhibition (Australia). David's recordings have been released through Gruenrekorder (DE), Green Field Recordings (PT), and Impulsive Habitat (PT), among others.

In his role as Academic Fellow at LCI Melbourne, Prescott-Steed coordinates the Contextual Studies program. His scholarly publications include "Feedback in a Looping System: Heuretic Pedagogy and Experimental Music" Textshop Experiments, no. 4 (2018); "We Are in an Image of the Subterranean Now: Making New Memories of Underground Space," Textshop Experiments, no. 3 (2017); Intersections of Creative Praxis and Urban Exploration, The Journal for Artistic Research, no. 9 (2015); "Invitation to Reading: Tactical Music in the Design-Arts Theory Classroom," in The Atrium: A Journal of Academic Voices (2015); "Frostbite On My Feet: Representations of Walking in Black Metal Visual Culture" Helvete: A Journal of Black Metal Theory, no. 1 (2013); and "A New Frontier for Visual Culture: Thoughts on the Production and Consumption of Digital Deep-Sea Imagery," KINEMA: A Journal for Film and Audiovisual Media (2012). Prescott-Steed's first book, The Psychogeography of Urban Architecture, was published in 2013 by Brown Walker Press (US).

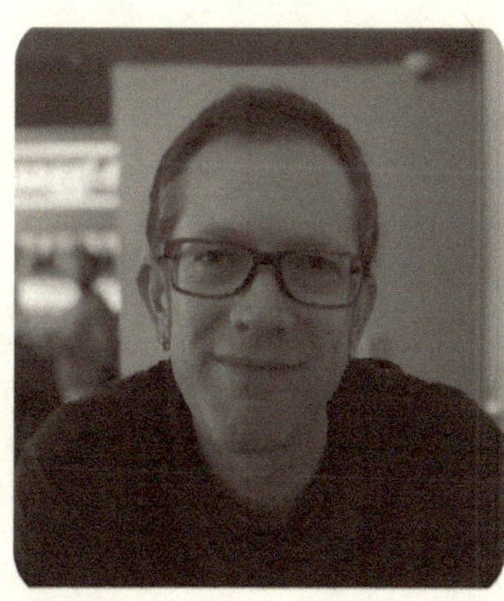

Photo of the author by Julie Borninkhof. Used by permission.

www.ingramcontent.com/pod-product-compliance
Lightning Source LLC
LaVergne TN
LVHW050958080826
845145LV00009B/2352

* 9 7 8 1 6 4 3 1 7 0 7 5 6 *